PRAISE FOR *LEAD WITH BALANCE*

"Every corporate CEO, university president, or person with a hectic lifestyle (which includes us all) should pause for a moment and read Lead with Balance: How to Master the Art of Work-Life Balance. *Just picking up the book makes you stop and reflect on how we are living our lives and, more importantly, how we should be living to optimize our well-being."*

Matthew D. Shank, PhD
President, Marymount University

"Donnie is the real deal when it comes to work-life balance. Donnie has lived it, learned from it, researched it, taught it, and now written about it, and we are the benefactors. We all know what we should be doing to balance our work and life, but few rarely translate 'should' to 'actual.' Donnie shares with all of us practical examples and stories that we can all learn from. As a fellow author and father of six children and four grandsons, I truly understand the importance of what Donnie has written about and am hopeful that readers will take his message to heart!"

Randy H. Nelson
Author of the #1 Amazon international best seller, The Second Decision: The Qualified Entrepreneur

"The author's passion on how to apply WLB into our lives shines through his teachings. The reason why Donnie's book is so valuable is that it reminds us of the gray area we often ignore in life, which is balance. He takes you on a remarkable journey, questioning your WLB. As a millennial, this Gen X-er knows what we want and is trying to teach others the same."

Khalida Ayoub, MHS
Lead Advisor of Health Care Division
Orange County, California

"Donnie Hutchinson takes a workplace issue facing all employees these days head on. He gives solid personal examples of the benefits of establishing and maintaining a healthy work-life balance. He also shares other poignant examples of where people aren't balanced. I feel his book will help people step back, reflect, assess, and hopefully balance themselves."

Steve Browne, SPHR
Executive Director of Human Resources
LaRosa's, Inc.

"This is a book everyone should read on work-life balance. But why should you—when there are so many books on this subject? Well here is why—it is full of real-life experiences and stories that will engage you, the reader, as well as provide you with simple steps of how to implement this in your life. It provides the pathway to making your life happier and more fulfilled.

In our fast-paced world where we are all doing more with less, we also know life is short. Why not take the time to read this, because I believe Donnie nailed it as they say in NY. Thank you Donnie for providing me with some great ways to make my life more fulfilled as well."

Patricia Tedesco
President of the Executive Training & Development Group, Inc.
Author of Quit Telling Me What To Do (How to Attract and Retain Key Talent)

"Donnie Hutchinson addresses a critically important topic that often lacks the attention it deserves. There is a direct correlation between organizational success and the personal fulfillment of our employees. I've had the good fortune to work for an organization that produces industry-leading results while cultivating an environment that values an employee's personal goals. Donnie writes with an honest and relatable voice, demonstrating the importance of work-life balance as a way to enhance our overall happiness."

Mark Lane
Senior Vice President, Sales
Berry

"*Ultimately a productive employee is not one that is working long, miserable hours. Donnie Hutchinson's research attests to the fact that employee productivity is directly linked to a balanced life. The 'senior leadership' in all companies, all industries, will benefit from reading this book.*"

Tim Brabender
Cochairman
McGohan Brabender

"*Hutch had integrated work-life balance before the term ever surfaced. I would not be surprised if he coined the phrase. As one with first-hand experience working under his leadership many years ago, I can attest to the fact this guy is a work-life balance champion. He put achieving his managers, and employees, work-life balance needs as a company objective. He led by example and taught us how we could be equally successful in our professional and personal lives.* Lead with Balance *changes your perspective on life and your perspective on how to achieve optimal success for your business and those you lead. You owe it to your family, your organization, and yourself to read this book!*"

Ray Barry
Managing Partner
Stevens and Stevens Business Records Management & Shred Link
Greenville, SC

"Lead with Balance will cause you to reflect and determine what you value in life. If you want to learn how to integrate work-life balance into your life and the lives of those you lead, then Lead with Balance is a must read for you and your management team. Follow the recommendations in this book and you will find yourself more productive, happier, and operating with a greater sense of well-being. If you are leading an organization, have your team read this book and discover the boomerang effects of balanced professionals."

Rusty Shelton
Founder
Shelton Interactive - Part of the Advantage Family

LEAD
WITH
BALANCE

LEAD
WITH
BALANCE

How to Master Work-Life Balance
in an Imbalanced Culture

DONNIE HUTCHINSON

Published by Advantage, Charleston, South Carolina.
Member of Advantage Media Group.

ADVANTAGE is a registered trademark and the Advantage colophon is a trademark of Advantage Media Group, Inc.

Printed in the United States of America.

ISBN: 978-1-59932-662-7
LCCN: 2016941020

Book design by Matthew Morse.

This publication is designed to provide accurate and authoritative information in regard to the subject matter covered. It is sold with the understanding that the publisher is not engaged in rendering legal, accounting, or other professional services. If legal advice or other expert assistance is required, the services of a competent professional person should be sought.

Advantage Media Group is proud to be a part of the Tree Neutral® program. Tree Neutral offsets the number of trees consumed in the production and printing of this book by taking proactive steps such as planting trees in direct proportion to the number of trees used to print books. To learn more about Tree Neutral, please visit **www.treeneutral.com.** To learn more about Advantage's commitment to being a responsible steward of the environment, please visit **www.advantagefamily.com/green**

Advantage Media Group is a publisher of business, self-improvement, and professional development books and online learning. We help entrepreneurs, business leaders, and professionals share their Stories, Passion, and Knowledge to help others Learn & Grow. Do you have a manuscript or book idea that you would like us to consider for publishing? Please visit **advantagefamily.com** or call **1.866.775.1696.**

For Marlene:
Thank you for your love and support.

For Rachel, Donnie, Gabriella, and Hannah:
Always strive to live with passion and balance during
your journey through life.

TABLE OF CONTENTS

MISSION

The mission of this book is to teach leaders, managers, and employees how to integrate work-life balance into their lives. Work-life balance is something I've always practiced in my early career, consulting work, teaching, and personal life. The new definition of leadership will be maximizing the workforce's well-being, happiness, and productivity through a balanced life. This "new genre" leadership approach will bring greater results to organizations, communities, employees, families, and America.

ACKNOWLEDGMENTS

T his work would not have been possible without the number of people that have helped me along this journey of work-life balance. I'm sincerely grateful, and many heartfelt thanks go out . . .

- To my students at University of Dayton: your passion for work-life balance and the encouragement you gave me to begin writing will always be remembered.
- To my fellow learners and instructors at University of Phoenix: you have been a source of knowledge and inspiration throughout this journey.
- To my former employers that supported my work-life balance philosophy and for allowing me to create and demonstrate a new style of leadership.
- To my clients, coworkers, and friends that have allowed me to use their stories to illustrate the importance of work-life balance.

- To those that have endorsed this book: your belief in me and this work-life balance movement will always be remembered.

- To all of the great people at Advantage Media: your guidance and support brought this idea to fruition.

- To my parents, for creating the foundation for my life's journey. Mom, the subtitle begins with *"How to . . ."*— now you know all those trips to the library when I was young were meaningful.

- To my wonderful children, Rachel, Donnie, Gabriella, and Hannah, for all of the great moments and memories we have shared and are creating through our journey in life. I especially thank you for our one-on-one, *couch time* discussions that help guide us into becoming the best we can be. A special thanks to Rachel for your outstanding editing skills and contributions to this work.

- To my beautiful wife, Marlene, for your excellent content suggestions and guidance throughout the book-writing process. Thank you for your love, support, and for teaching me the art of relationships.

- To God, for with you, all things are possible.

A WORD FROM THE AUTHOR

This is a book on the importance of balance in everyday life—in your own life and in your employees' lives. The pressures of our current culture and the constant focus on the bottom line means we are frequently overcompensating in certain areas and neglecting others, which leads to problems in both our personal and professional lives. One imbalance leads to another imbalance, which leads to unhappiness. Maybe we're working so hard we neglect our family, forget to eat well and exercise, or push ourselves to the brink, which makes us overlook time needed to go to church or meditate. This imbalance has a negative impact on us and our relationships at home and at work and in other areas in our lives.

Balanced people and employees are not only happier but also more productive. We need to get back on track and take the time to stop, reflect, and understand our needs and priorities, and we need to find careers that allow for that balance. This book is for all those who feel that something isn't right and they need to get back on track with balancing their priorities. It is also a wake-up call to leaders who want to consider these factors to ensure their employees are as productive and happy as possible so they can reach their full potential. As a leader, your goal should be to make sure your employees are their best—and balance is the key ingredient.

In this book, I will illustrate my points by providing examples and case studies of organizations and people whom I have worked with, studied, taught, and known, including associates, clients, acquaintances, and students. I will share how my overall approach to a balanced life enlightens my personal life, speaking engagements, consulting work, and teaching.

Each chapter will contain assessment tools and other resources to help you begin a journey on reflecting, resetting, and rebalancing as an individual and as a leader in your organization. I encourage you, my readers, to have a pen in hand or a stylist for the e-book. Jot down your ideas in the margins and call-out boxes. Some of the best thoughts are the first ones that come to mind. Read, write your reflections, and enjoy the journey to balance your imbalance.

INTRODUCTION

A Balanced Life

Many of us are living and perpetuating a culture of imbalance to meet the needs of "main street" and Wall Street. Much of what we do as employees and leaders in organizations is to improve the revenue and profitability while frequently sacrificing our personal lives and those we love the most.

Take my friend James, for example. He's nearing fifty years old and has been an accountant for twenty-five years. He is married to Nicole, and they have two children in high school. James spent numerous hours at the office each week for as many years as I can remember. He often missed his kids' athletic and school activities because he was not willing to take time away from the office. He often reminded me that becoming a partner in an accounting firm was the goal, and it was about loyalty and billable time, things you can't address if you take time off work to attend your child's activities with your spouse. James would say, "My wife will be there, as she always is, showing our parental support." Yes, Nicole was there, usually sitting with some of the other solo parents whose spouses could not make it to the 7:00 p.m. game.

James is a very nice and likable person. I got to know him through a men's group at our church. We used to meet weekly, for years, at the local brew pub on Wednesday nights from 7:00 p.m. to 8:30 p.m. until many of the members' lives appeared to get too busy for them to meet. The group consisted of about eight guys who were all married and had children. We used this time to talk about life's struggles, such as balancing the needs of our families and work. We often felt that the hour and a half we men spent together on those nights was worth a fortune. We all energized each other and helped each other feel we were not alone in this battle over time—everyone except for James. He frequently mentioned how he worked long hours and how he had not been the best husband to his wife or father to his children. I could see the sadness in his eyes every week he showed up for the men's group.

A few years went by and, one day, I ran into James. He had been an athletic guy, but he had put on fifty pounds. He looked tired. "Hey, Hutch," he said to me, "aren't you going to congratulate me?" He had made partner at his accounting firm the year before.

I said, "Congratulations my friend. Now that you are a partner, have you been able to work less hours and spend more time with your family?" James had been working between sixty and seventy hours each week for at least ten years.

He replied, "No, not yet, because my billable rates are so good I just can't give up the extra money. I even work on Sundays now."

I stopped seeing him with his family at church. I wondered how much anyone would have to earn to willingly stop abandoning spouse, children, religious practice, and personal well-being. I began to wonder when James had last taken his spouse out on a date or watched his children play sports or gone to church. I hadn't seen him in months. What I did not wonder about was whether or not he was taking care of himself by eating a balanced diet and exercising. The tiredness in his face from the extra fifty pounds he was carrying around answered that question.

Do you know someone like James? Are you James? How do you think this story will end? Will all his work mean that his wife will leave him and they will get a divorce? Will his neglect of his health result in a heart attack, and will this be what finally forces him to slow down? Or will he hit the reset button and turn his life around by working fewer hours, spending more time with his spouse and children, and beginning to eat well and exercise regularly? Will his employer be surprised to find him more productive at work while working fewer hours? You'll find out how James's future turns out later in the book.

My purpose in writing this book is to teach readers and leaders just like you to bring balance into your hectic lives and more productivity into your work. This is a book for people who feel they could be happier in their careers and personal lives. You will experience greater well-being and happiness in your life. Those closest to you will also benefit from your rebalancing your behaviors and your schedule. Can you imagine how a balanced life could bring greater satisfaction to everyone in your personal and professional life? Why wait to take action? Please get your pen out and respond to the following prompt.

REFLECTION BOX

Write a note to yourself in this box, briefly describing how a balanced life would bring greater satisfaction to people in your personal and professional life.

The Business Case for a Balanced Life

Beyond the personal reasons, a business case can also be made for a balanced life. Millennials (born after 1980) are seeking opportunities that offer a more balanced lifestyle (work-from-home jobs, casual offices, etc.). As a result, a balanced workplace is already something that is in progress. The opportunity to frame our workplace cultures differently is huge. If leaders don't stay on top of this trend, they'll lose good employees and business.

A majority of managers and leaders in the workplace today are baby boomers (born 1946–1964) and Generation Xers (born 1965–1980). Many live a life of work, work, and more work, while their families, friends, health, and sometimes, religious practice, have taken a back seat to putting in more time at the office. Millennials have watched their baby boomer parents sacrifice many family and social opportunities. This generation of employees will soon be the largest generation in the workforce. Remember they are currently evaluating their work culture to see if it meets their needs. They realized their parents, who begrudgingly stayed late at the office, year after year, lost sight of balance while they pursued happiness in the wrong place.

REFLECT, RESET, AND REBALANCE

If you feel your life is out of balance, the first step begins with forgiving yourself. No one is perfect. I advocate learning the skill of self-forgiveness. Guilt is a difficult emotion that is best fought with love and forgiveness. After all, life is a juggling act. Balance is the key to well-being, happiness, and success. The balance of a career with the needs of family, faith, and health will ebb and flow. There are times when we must work late at the office. When a family or close friend falls ill, we stop what we are doing and rush to their bedside.

There are other times when a life event automatically rebalances us—for example, news of a severe health condition that needs immediate attention. However, in our normal daily life we shouldn't focus for too long on one aspect of our life rather than giving equal attention to all aspects. Otherwise, we will see negative consequences.

Our lives and what we include in our life balancing formula should be recognized for what they are: a living system. What we choose to do and when we choose to do it has an effect on the things we choose not to do. All components of our life are intricately linked to each other. It is also important to understand the overall objective of our life: our desire for well-being and happiness.

IMBALANCE PERPETUATED

Organizations perpetuate our propensity for imbalance. Many organizations still treat workers as commodities. While they may not like to use the word *commodity*, it's what leadership has taught us over several decades. For example, Wall Street companies and some mainstreet firms define an effective organization as one where the leader exploits the worker under the guise of motivational and improvement strategies. In other words, what is the latest and greatest motivational strategy or technique to get more production out of our current team? Have you ever heard of doing more with less? What does doing more with less mean to most people? Less time for family, friends, good nutrition, exercise, and your religious practice.

Corporate leaders often ignore the different external forces fighting for their employee's attention. Many leadership scholars define corporations as open systems where everything is interconnected with three competing forces fighting for attention. The first of these forces is company metrics, which often come in the form of revenue, profit, quality, customer satisfaction, and so on. Many leaders and managers believe the company's welfare is the only item that needs attention.

Second, the external environment weighs in with various claims on our attention. A good example of an external force that imposes its authority is that of employment laws, which can have major impacts on an employer's human resources (HR) department. They can affect a wide range of functions from employee benefits to hiring and termination practices, requiring HR personnel to overhaul their policies and practices.

The last and most important force is that of individuals' personal goals and wishes, which operate as an opposing force. For instance, new mothers and fathers probably want to work less and be home more with their family since they are learning to rebalance their home and professional lives. Another example is a single mother who would love to participate in her fifth grader's field day at the local elementary school, yet she can't take an extra hour for lunch without it being frowned upon. Are you aware of the opposing forces fighting for your attention? If you are a manager, are you aware of any differing interests seeking your employee's attention?

LOST SIGHT OF "WHY" WE ARE WORKING

We've lost sight of why we work: the goal of well-being and happiness. Americans rank thirteenth among happiest nations, according to the 2016 World Happiness Report. Since the US has the world's largest economy, it clearly shows money does not buy happiness. Why do other countries, including third-world developing countries, score higher on happiness than American citizens? We work for many reasons, and one of those is money. We work longer and longer hours to make more money. We do this because we have been indoctrinated into the pursuit of profit and return on investment—Wall Street's only metric in deciding if a company is good or bad.

In our fast-paced culture, there's little time for reflection, and we've suffered. Technology has grayed the playing field of work and home. But ironically, just as technology is partly to blame for the accelerating pace of our workload and never-ending workday, there are also signs that it might help us reset and get back in balance—for example, apps that tell us to disengage our social media or e-mail. Health-tracking devices now exist to help us manage our exercise routine, and scheduling apps can help us schedule family time or a date with our spouse or a friend.

While starting with a focus on personal balance is a good step, it isn't enough. We need to think bigger, and as leaders, we need to start making sure our employees are living balanced lives as well. This breakthrough concept of balance will provide employers with more satisfied employees, improved productivity, and lower costs. Happy employees are the most productive team members. Truly caring for your workforce is an example of leadership with authenticity. Helping your employees live a balanced life for the betterment of their well-being while benefiting from increased productivity is a win-win situation, not exploitation.

All signs point to this change happening now. We can no longer run away from it. Young people, older people, millennials—many people are already asking for it, and if they can't get it, they go out on their own and find their own way. As leaders, we don't just have a responsibility; we face an urgent necessity to put systems into place that allow for more balance in our employees' lives.

I see this growing drive for employee balance every day. As a professor who is also a student pursuing a PhD in organizational leadership, I see this manifesting in my students and my research.

The millennial students completely connect with the philosophy of balance and have demonstrated a call to action to find their "fit" with the employer of their choice. As a consultant to top-level executives in nearly every industry, I see this drive for balance having a direct impact on the lives of leaders, employees, and families while positively contributing to the bottom line. I work with people who love their employees and want to help them thrive by helping them find balance in their individual lives. My speaking and consulting practice provides me an environment where I can introduce academic concepts and bring these to life in the real world while seeing people, families, and organizations benefit. In my career, I have worked as a business developer, VP of sales, COO, organizational coach, and president.

The business development position early in my career at Xerox, in the early '90s, provided the initial spark that made me aware of the benefits of living a balanced life. As a member of a sales team, I noticed our organizational culture encouraged showing up after work at the local watering hole. Over the course of a year, I observed that two of the married sales reps always hung out with the singles crowd. I wondered whether their spouses were very upset with them and whether their children wondered when they would be home. At that very moment, I recognized what an imbalanced life looked like.

It did not take me long to figure out that the end game for these folks would probably not be a pretty picture. Not only did they work long hours but they also focused all of their energies and excitement on themselves and their careers. While they won many awards and benefited from large bonuses, they neglected their duties as loving spouse and parent. They also went silent on faith because they had no time to fit it into their busy schedules. One of my teammates, also a friend of mine, neglected his health. He was overweight, yet he continued to live an unhealthy lifestyle. Sad to say, five years after I started working with this team, one member was divorced and the other suffered a heart attack that changed his life.

What good is success at work when everything else in your life suffers? What good is being in the top 10 percent of wage earners if you end up divorced, estranged from your children, or dead? I thought there had to be a better formula for success. Wall Street's measurement of success is profitability and return on investment. I knew there had to be a better answer—one benefiting all stakeholders.

Thankfully, I also worked with people who demonstrated a balanced life, and their definition of success was one I couldn't forget. Several married team members with children were miraculously able to find time to be very effective sales professionals, spouses, friends, and parents. They were able to close the big sale and attend the soccer game at 4:00 p.m. on the same day. They prioritized what was important in their lives. It was obvious they valued the benefits of eating a well-balanced diet and exercising frequently. Over the years, I listened to several of their faith stories and learned that their faith was intertwined with their family and professional lives. I decided, at that point, to seek a life of balance rather than one of imbalance. My definition of a successful life was going to include four pillars: family/close relationships, career, faith, and healthy living habits.

My career eventually turned toward organizational and leadership development consulting. This happened after I was able to demonstrate that leading an organization with a balanced life approach worked better than any other motivational tactics. Caring for the people around me and their well-being became a staple in my leadership plan, both at work and at home.

Yet, as I mentioned before, balance ebbs and flows. I had balance in work, health, faith, and with my children but not with my spouse.

When people spend too much time in one or more areas of their daily lives, something usually gives. In my case, the imbalance led to divorce.

Trying to live a balanced life took on new meaning for me, as a recent divorcee, leader of a company, and single parent of four children. After a few years of being a single, full-time dad, I remarried. My second marriage brought a new dimension of balance to me, one that includes spending quality time with each other while balancing all of our other roles in life. She has taught me how adult relationships are supposed to work: with love, laughter, and time for each other.

I have been a practitioner, not an expert, of living a balanced life for more than twenty years. I strive to head in the true north direction for balance, yet I often find myself needing to reflect, reset, and rebalance. This approach provides me with the needed course corrections to get back on track. The contemporary philosophy of living a balanced life and my efforts to help organizations adopt a balanced-life approach in the workplace are what provide the fuel for my consulting and teaching practice. I practice what I teach, which is the definition of authentic leadership. I have inspired and taken action to help my managers and employees lead a more balanced life. Helping employees achieve greater well-being and happiness has taken corporate social responsibility to a new level.

I am on a mission. My career purpose is helping leaders, managers, and employees perform their best and thrive, and balance is key to this. I speak at colleges, corporations, seminars, and industry and association events, and I speak through this book, in which I discuss what I have found to be the most fulfilling aspects of my career.

Wall Street's definition of leadership—maximizing profits regardless of the cost to the well-being of employees and communities—needs to become yesterday's definition. The new definition of leadership will be maximizing the workforce's well-being, happiness, and productivity through a balanced life. This *new genre* leadership approach will bring greater results to the organization, communities, employees, and their families. Believe it or not, it will also benefit Wall Street in the long run because we will become a more productive society.

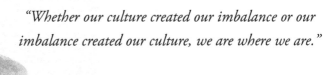

"Whether our culture created our imbalance or our imbalance created our culture, we are where we are."

CHAPTER 1

A Culture of Imbalance: How Did We Get Here?

need you to make a choice: your job or your child's wedding? This may be an extreme example, yet this was the news my friend Julie received from her manager, Ryan. She was getting her doctorate to enhance her accounting degree and skills. She was employed in a medium-sized company where she had been an in-house accountant for eighteen years. She received this news from her boss, Ryan, the newly appointed chief financial officer (CFO), after she had submitted her request for a vacation:

"Excuse me," Julie said. "You want me to what?"

She had heard her boss correctly.

"You cannot take the last week off in July for your son's wedding, because we are implementing the new accounting software that week," Ryan reiterated. "You are going to need to choose between attending your son's wedding or staying employed at this company."

Julie broke out in tears. "Ryan, this wedding has been planned for two years. The software conversion was planned by you last month. Can't we work together to find an alternative solution?"

"No," Ryan said. "There's no other option. You need to choose between work and the wedding."

Julie was furious. "Well, I guess I will need to find a new job!"

Does Johnny Paycheck's song "Take This Job and Shove It" come to mind? Fictitious? No, unfortunately, this is a true story that happened in the spring of 2015. Julie told her story to all of her classmates. Jaws dropped, and then her classmates joined in with similar stories of managers making people choose between work and family or work and one's faith.

I am happy to say Julie had the time of her life at her son's wedding. She was very proud of herself for leaving a leader and organizational culture of individual destruction. She has been happily employed for six months in a company where she is valued as a human being. She says putting in the extra effort and time for an employer who cares about her happens naturally.

What's going on in our culture that this happens so frequently? What's it like to be an American employee or manager right now, in this climate? Let's look at some of the details of the current state of our imbalanced culture to set the stage for the rest of the book.

Statistics and Ramifications on Imbalance

According to a 2014 Gallup poll, full-time American employees work an average of forty-seven hours per week, 18 percent of Americans work over sixty hours per week, and 21 percent work between fifty and fifty-nine hours per week. How many people do you know who work forty hours per week? If you know some, then others must be working fifty-four hours per week just to get the average to forty-seven. Is that too much or too little? Well, the Netherlands, Denmark, Norway, Switzerland, Australia, and Sweden average a much shorter workweek than the USA does, and those countries are higher on the world index of happiest citizens.

According to the Centers for Disease Control and Prevention, 34 percent of Americans are overweight, and 35 percent are obese. In other words, two-thirds of the US population have an unhealthy body mass index. This is not a recipe for increasing productivity in the American workforce. Being overweight or obese is associated with coronary heart disease, high blood pressure, stroke, type 2 diabetes, cancer, osteoarthritis, and sleep apnea. None of these diseases are welcomed. We leaders need to strategically focus on our people to lead them into establishing some positive self-care habits, such as proper diet and exercise.

American marriages fail nearly 50 percent of the time, according to the American Psychological Association. This high ratio peaked in the 1970s and 1980s when both parents were working full-time in the workforce. Double incomes created a new type of imbalance in family management: who's picking up the kids, and what will we be having for dinner tonight? Oftentimes, as many of us know, marriages can end up in divorce, which leads to another balancing challenge in our culture: single parenting.

Single and divorced parents have extra challenges while trying to balance the struggles of career, family, faith, and health. Managers may unrealistically expect single and divorced employees to function just as a two-parent family does, even though the other parent isn't usually in the picture to pick up the baby from daycare or be available after school when the children come home. Single parents may feel overwhelmed by the responsibility of balancing their parental duties, maintaining a career, and keeping up with normal household burdens. In addition, single parents often feel guilty about their children's situation, so they often overcompensate by spending more time with their children and less at work. They have already given up their personal health time. Eating a well-balanced meal and finding time for exercise is nearly impossible.

Attending a religious service may be difficult in today's culture of imbalance. It wasn't always like this. Ask your parents or grandparents if they used to shop on Sundays. The answer will be a resounding no. Nothing was open back in those days. Stores closed so workers could spend time at home and attend a religious service if they chose to do so.

Do you require your employees to work on Sundays? Chick-Fil-A sure doesn't. That's the wildly successful fast-food franchise that Wall Street said would fail because it chose not to be open for business on Sundays. The founder, Truett Cathy, believes all franchised Chick-Fil-A operators and their employees should have an opportunity to rest, spend time with family and friends, and worship if they choose to do so. That's why all Chick-Fil-A restaurants are closed on Sundays. Cathy frequently cites this policy as the reason for their success. How many businesses do you know with the same Chick-Fil-A philosophy?

Ramifications of Disengaged Employees

So what are the ramifications of having a culture of imbalance? A 2015 Gallup study revealed over two-thirds of American employees and managers are not engaged in their jobs. At some point in their career, one in two of those employees leave their job in an attempt to rebalance their life. People quit managers not companies. Why? Bad managers make employees feel unhappy, and that unhappiness follows them home, adding to their stress and negatively affecting their overall well-being.

There is an immediate need and value in helping your employees and managers to avoid derailments and to find balance in their careers, families, religion, and health. The pressures of our current culture and the constant focus on the bottom line means that we frequently overcompensate in certain areas and neglect others, which leads to problems in both our personal and professional lives. One imbalance leads to another imbalance, which leads to unhappiness, which leads to disengagement, which leads to lower productivity and commitment. All of this falls to the bottom line in a negative manner.

Never-Ending Workday

There once was a workday called nine to five. It later became known as eight to five. For some, it did not take long for the workday to mean 24/7/365. The advancements in technology have allowed employees to be available twenty-four hours per day, seven days per week, 365 days per year. Constantly checking and operating our smartphones has become a society norm. It is very common to see couples, families, and wait staff in restaurants frequently checking and using their phone while they are in the midst of company or family. We have become a slave to our phones and to those who want our attention.

Have you ever known people who wanted to stay late at work because they felt it impressed the boss? I certainly have, and it was difficult to watch, especially when the boss was impressed with that employee's perceived commitment. Many bosses define working late hours as loyalty. However, there is another side to that coin. Most of these people who work long hours are out of balance. They do not wish to go home at a reasonable time. They create the Parkinson's law for themselves. That is, they stretch the time it takes to complete their daily tasks to match the amount of time they wish to spend at the office. Give people eight hours to complete a task, and they will complete it in eight hours. Give people ten hours to complete the same task, and they will take ten hours to complete it.

I have worked with many people who don't always take their allotted vacation time each year. I have seen many people take their laptop on vacation with them and end up getting pulled away from their family or friends to complete a task or two for their employer. Most people like to feel needed, but recharging the batteries is a foundational element for sustainable success. Do you remember Stephen Covey's seventh habit of "sharpening the saw"? Covey encouraged us to balance and renew our resources, energy, and health to create a sustainable and effective lifestyle.

The never-ending workday definitely extends into personal time, even when we choose to have a few beers with coworkers. Granted, this is a great time and one that I have participated in for many years and still do. However, it's worth considering what this workday extension costs the spouse or children if it becomes too lengthy or occurs too often.

The workweek is no longer defined as Monday through Friday. As you know, many people work Saturdays and Sundays in addition to the old norm of five days per week. In our current culture of imbalance, this work commitment is rewarded, despite the science that shows productivity plummets after forty hours of work and despite the fact that commitment to a longer workweek takes people away from family, friends, faith, and exercise. The never-ending workday focuses on *human doings* versus *human beings*.

No True Divide between Work and Personal Life

Turning off your office light or punching a time card is no longer the "off" switch that separates work from personal time. We often believe there is a separation between work and personal time. However, technology has not only blurred the lines; technology has interwoven them. For example, many employees use one or more social media sites for personal enjoyment. On many social websites we can tag pictures and add a humorous caption. We are not using company computers or company time; we are simply having fun with social media friends. However, is your social media content acceptable to your employer's social media policy? You know the one—the one that states you cannot post or contribute to anything on the Internet that could put your company in a bad light. There is no true divide between work and personal life. You may think you have personal space, but it is often restricted.

Our culture of imbalance treats religious conversations and behaviors in the workplace as offensive and distasteful. Why can't they be treated as an opportunity to learn and grow from one another? I am not speaking about learning to simply be tolerant of others. I am speaking about going a step beyond: learning to *accept* people for who they are as human beings. Many people have some degree of spirituality within them. The artificial divide between work and personal life stifles our learning about each other and learning to accept and appreciate our differences.

Here's another divide: Why are women (and men) expected to return to work immediately after having a baby as if nothing had happened? Does any manager really believe that life outside the office is normal for that new parent? Expecting a new parent to function as if nothing has changed in their life will eventually create problems and may be considered cold and insensitive. Why not be proactive on the front end and give the employee flexibility?

FAMILY TIME AND TECHNOLOGY

The last time I checked, cable television offered more than five hundred channels. The average American home has 2.8 TVs per household. What once offered a chance for the family to gather together has now segregated the family into the "PG," "R," and "sports" rooms. Family members will text other members in a different room to see how well they like their show. Television and technology often replace real interaction. I find it amusing and sad to see a family sitting around a restaurant table, all on their smartphones, conducting business, engaging in social media, or reading the news headlines instead of interacting with one another in live verbal and nonverbal communication. Essentially, our human conversations are being replaced by screen time.

There is hope, however: encouragement from a balanced millennial. My wife, an avid screen user, along with her mother, recently visited her daughters, ages nineteen and twenty-three. Three of these four ladies (grandma excluded) agree they spend a large amount of time on their smartphones. However, this group has a mastery of face-to-face conversation. Yes, this means they are a talkative bunch. The youngest lady in the group, my stepdaughter Jordan, suggested they do what she and her friends do when they go out to lunch or dinner. They gather their cell phones together, click on the airplane mode, and place the phones on an empty chair or in the middle of the table. I thought that was an outstanding idea. This proactive approach allows you to give others your undivided attention when they're speaking to you. Don't we all like to have people pay attention to our words and facial expressions when we are speaking, instead of texting or reading the latest Facebook post?

HEALTH NEGLECT

It's as easy as one, two, three: calories in, calories burned, and sleep to rejuvenate the mind and body. Well, the formula may be accurate, but it's not easy to manage our health in today's culture. We Americans eat out an average of 4.2 times per week, up significantly from a generation ago. Not only do we consume more calories eating out, but we also forgo spending quality time together, preparing meals, and eating at the family dining table. You remember what that was, the place where everyone gathers to give thanks, share a meal, and talk to each other about their day? We are running hard all day and night and try our best to catch up with our spouse and kids before it is time to turn out the lights for the night.

So how do most of us attempt to recapture more of the family time that slips away from us on a daily basis? We sleep less. According to the 2014 Gallup study, 40 percent of Americans sleep six hours or less per night. The American Medical Association continues to advocate that we should get between seven and nine hours of sleep per night to rejuvenate our minds and bodies. What happens to the body when we get less sleep? It stores more fat, and we gain weight. What? Getting less sleep actually causes weight gain? According to the experts at WebMD, the body cannot completely regulate itself on less than seven and a half hours of sleep.

How in the world am I supposed to fit in exercise when I am spending all of these hours at the office? We are already eating several dinners out to save time. I am getting less sleep because I am trying to prioritize my work-life balance by staying up later to finish my unfinished tasks. Exercise? Yeah, sure. I will think about putting that into the schedule tomorrow. Does tomorrow ever come?

Once in a while, change *does* come, but for some, it is with juice cleanses coupled with extreme diet or exercise. Have you ever known people to set themselves up for failure by completely depriving themselves of food or attempting to train as a professional athlete does? Millions do each year, especially around New Year's resolutions time. They inevitably fail, or even worse, starve themselves or strain themselves. Our culture only seems to understand extremes. Balance is critical for success in the big picture of life as well as the smaller areas in our lives.

DISAPPEARING REFLECTION

What happened to reflection? Remember that thing you used to do as a child, lying in bed, staring up at the ceiling, reflecting on what went well and what could have gone better? If you are trying to head true north, how can you if you go off the path by simply a few degrees? People are on autopilot, often missing their destination because they don't pause, reflect, and course-correct. Our busy lives in this culture of imbalance cause us to not look at our lives honestly and closely. We work, work, and work to burnout. We've lost sight of why we are really working: happiness and well-being.

Are you really working for well-being and happiness? I know many people who say they are happy when they are working, which may be a true statement yet not a complete one. Happiness has evolved from that untouchable "thing" that we are pursuing to an actual science. Happiness, along with overall well-being, is an up-and-coming academic field called positive psychology. Martin Seligman, author of *Flourish* and one of the founding members of positive psychology, shares with his readers that well-being and happiness can be systematically achieved. It is important to note that money does not buy happiness once you meet your basic needs of food, shelter, and water. As the country music song by Chris Jansen says, "I know everybody says money can't buy me happiness. But it can buy me a boat; it could buy me a truck to pull it." It can buy things, but it cannot buy happiness.

In order to have sustainable well-being, which includes happiness, Seligman posits we need to have five elements in our life. They are (1) positive emotion (happiness), (2) engagement, (3) relationships, (4) meaning, and (5) accomplishment. Positive emotion is, simply, joy. Engagement happens when you are so engulfed in a task or project that you lose track of time. I remember times in my childhood when I was fully engaged. I would sit at the kitchen table building a model sports car. I would sit there for hours until I had the perfect model to display in my bedroom. When are you so engaged in a task or project that you lose track of time? Figuring out those moments can help you restore balance to your life and find your passion.

REFLECTION BOX

Write a note to yourself in this box, briefly describing the type of project you get engaged with.

Relationships are critical to well-being. We are social creatures and live in communities, both geographical and web based. Our need to connect to people is important, even if some of us have a tendency to be reclusive. Achieving *meaningfulness* fulfills our human need to do something that is "bigger" than we are. We want to feel our work is important and meaningful. In fact, many organizations state their "purpose" on their websites. Working and living for a purpose helps us achieve meaningfulness. Accomplishment is pursued for its own sake, even though it may not bring any positive emotion or meaningfulness. It is simply the joy of pursuing achievement.

Let's reflect for a moment to see if well-being/happiness is our number-one goal. Why do you work? Yes, you can derive feelings of accomplishment from working, and you can enjoy work relationships, and so on. Are you earning a living to support yourself and your family? Yes, you work to earn money and to gain important benefits such as health insurance for yourself and your family. But why do you want to provide for yourself and your family? Do you want to meet everyone's basic needs and then some? Of course you do—and I do too. The question then becomes whether, if you work so much it takes away from family or close relationships, you have become out of balance. Will your true north objective of finding well-being and happiness be achieved by spending more time at the office?

REFLECTION BOX

Well-being and happiness: If you are experiencing, or would like to experience, well-being and happiness in your day-to-day life, what does, or would, that look like?

The Cultural Shift Is Happening Now

The call for balance has never been more important or timely for us as individuals and leaders. We can't shift back to the old days of nine to five with no communication after we turn our office lights off. There's a better way, and our workplace is going to have to reflect this shift. Millennials want something different. According to the Intelligence Group, 88 percent of millennials want work-life integration, and 74 percent want flexible work schedules. In essence, they want balance.

I recently taught a three-credit-hour class on organizational behavior, on Monday evenings at the University of Dayton. I had thirteen US and thirteen international students in my class. During the third week of class, I added a ten-minute presentation on how I strive to live a balanced life of faith, family, career, and health. I shared with my students how these four elements play a major role in my personal life and my life as a business leader.

My minilecture on a balanced life was intertwined with a lecture on finding your "fit" in an organization. I encouraged my junior-level students to consider their up-and-coming career interviews their senior year to be a two-way street. I mentioned this to them every week to plant the seed of asking questions about the company culture to see if they are a good "fit" for that particular organization. It was important for me to help them start thinking about what was important to them. For an extra credit question, I asked, "What do you see as important elements or traits to help guide and manage your future?"

Here are a few answers from my millennial students:

- The first and most important thing to me is family (international student).

- Relationships are so important to value, and you should take care of them (US student).
- If you don't take care of your health, everything else will not matter (international student).
- I want to have a job that allows me to go to church on Sundays (US student).
- It's important to have balance and be healthy for those who love you (international student).
- Faith is more important than career because if I lose my faith I will hate my career (international student).

The most heart-tugging comment I received was from a student named David. He shared the following comment with me in March 2015:

Professor Hutch, you said your core values included faith, family, career, and health. I thought that sharing this with the class was a real example of what it takes to take on jobs in the "real world" as other students and myself define life after college. Your core values very much reflect my own. I may add friendship, but our values are very much the same. When I told my dad your core values, he said it was the answer to his prayers. He had been searching for a job and was on the fence about a job that would take two hours to drive to. He said this would negatively impact his faith and health, and he did not take the job. I felt responsible for him not taking a good job, but I think hearing what you had to say is exactly what he needed. So thank you, I am sure he would agree.

−David A.

Technology

We are already seeing the culture shift everywhere. Ironically, the thing that helped get us here is now helping us limit our smartphone addictions. There are apps such as Moment and Checky that help users become aware of their screen time to assist in behavioral change. Let's face it, we may tell ourselves and those we love that we don't have a problem with spending too much time on our smartphones. However, if we are honest with ourselves, as my University of Dayton students were honest with me, we would have to admit that we spend too much time checking our screens.

During one of my lectures, I noticed a student reading a text message. I paused and wondered if my students were aware they had a problem with spending too much time on their phone. I decided to take an impromptu survey with the twenty-six students in my class.

I asked, "How many of you feel you spend too much time on your smartphones?"

Amazingly, all twenty-six students raised their hands.

I said, "Wow! Really?"

One of the US students spoke up, "Yes, I spend more time on my phone than I do studying, and it is causing me problems with my grades."

A Chinese student spoke out, "I spend a lot of time tweeting to my friends in China, and I should be taking that time to make friends here on campus."

All of a sudden I realized these students were reaching out for help. I continued my dialogue with them and steered it toward potential solutions. One of the student leaders of the group talked about his struggles with screen time and also drew our attention to an app he was using that put a daily limit on his screen time. He said it was working for him, and he recommended others to try it.

With some help from these usage-limiting apps, we can all start making a positive shift toward balancing technology in our professional and social lives but only if we make the conscious effort and stick to it.

Globalization

As the workforce becomes more global, things are starting to change even more, and the values of other cultures are beginning to infuse our own. For example, my international students were all from China. They all stressed the importance of family in their core belief system. One student said, "The Chinese culture always puts filial devotion as a person's most important moral standard." Perhaps, this devotion can infuse itself into our US culture to help us reclaim the family dinner time. Luckily, we have a few employers who are listening and leading the change.

You may be thinking that I will talk about companies such as Google and HP. These large companies, although highly rated places to work, at the onset, actually contribute to the downward spiral of imbalance. You may ask how companies that have been voted as some of the greatest places to work contribute to an imbalanced life.

Well, it all started when tech companies wanted their employees to work around the clock to get a software package released. Employees started having a problem with finding time to take care of things they needed to get done in their personal lives, such as getting lunch, picking their child up at daycare, exercising, and getting their hair cut. Therefore, managers decided to install an in-house gourmet café serving free breakfasts, lunches, dinners, and midnight snacks. Daycare was now offered onsite as an employee benefit, along with haircuts, pedicures, and massages. Need a nap? Just use your swipe card to enter the napping room. What more could an employee ask for? Tech companies made the workplace feel better than home. Or did they? What about family, friends outside work, close relationships, religious worship, exercising with family and friends, eating family dinners or dining with a close friend? What happened to that part of their life? Remember one imbalance leads to another and another and so on.

The Real Change: Live like Millennials

Getting back to working forty hours per week, whether at a company location or at home, is being recognized by some leading companies as the best way to ensure employees' well-being and happiness and productivity in the workplace—a win-win for all involved.

You may think, *This guy's math does not add up. How can forty hours per week be more productive than sixty hours of work?* It is simply known as the law of diminishing returns. For each hour above forty hours worked per week, the marginal gain in productivity is about 25–30 percent. In other words, an extra hour of working does not equate to an extra hour of output. That extra hour will only deliver between fifteen and twenty minutes of output. This is because the energy level drops. This is why more accidents happen during overtime and long workweeks. Employee fatigue is one of the reasons why the forty-hour workweek became the standard. AlterNet's Sara Robinson, in her article titled "Bring Back the 40-Hour Work Week," cites a formula that is more than a hundred years old: eight hours of work, eight hours of social time, and eight hours of sleep. This is the standard that has been proven to give the greatest output.

I once worked for a leader who was adamant that the cost of overtime was the same as adding a new employee, and it was easier to have someone work overtime. His math was simple: overtime wages are equal to a new employee's straight time plus benefits. While, from a cost-accounting viewpoint, his formula is accurate, from a throughput standpoint—that is, how much work is being done and produced—he was wrong. The additional employee would be much more productive than the employee working overtime. Given the state of unemployment in the USA, it makes complete sense to bring the workweek back to forty hours and add employees to the team if needed. Costs are equal, yet throughput is greater!

Creating a work environment that embraces full energy at work while sending employees home after forty hours is an example of embracing balance and maximizing productivity. Another example is how the TSheets CEO, Matt Rissell, shows his love for his hundred-plus employees. He is an authentic, disciplined leader who focuses on the well-being and happiness of all individuals in all aspects of their lives. His technology firm simplifies employee time and attendance systems via smartphones. The company has been voted the number-one place to work in Idaho. It's easy to see Matt's passion for a work-life balance. Just look at one of his YouTube videos on the TSheets website. The feature *About the CEO* has a picture of Matt with his wife, three children, and their dog.

Matt agrees that balance includes juggling the pillars of his life, consisting of family, career, faith, and health. "Balance does not mean equal time for each area of my life," Matt says. He explains that he explained his need to devote more time to leading TSheets to his family and received their buy-in. "Balance actually consists of the ebb and flow of family, career, faith, and health," he says.

According to Matt, discipline and the acceptance that there is no perfect balance is what helps him feel balanced in life. His discipline consists of scheduling time with his wife and children to ensure he provides for their relationship needs. He also is very disciplined with his diet, and he exercises five times per week. Matt does not focus on balance. Rather, he focuses on what needs attention at a particular time. Given the fact that he is disciplined in his diet, exercise, and religious life, the ebbs and flows between family and work happen naturally and without issues for him.

Matt told me a story that demonstrates how well-being and love for his employees is met with action. One of Matt's employees—we will call him Dave—asked him for help. Dave was overweight and knew nothing about eating healthy food or exercising. He told Matt he was seeking advice from him because he had grown to respect the love Matt showed his employees. Matt's response to Dave's request for advice was, "Grab your coat."

Matt drove Dave to the grocery store, grabbed a shopping cart, and took Dave up and down each aisle. He educated Dave on where the healthy items were located in the grocery and pointed out items he felt Dave should avoid purchasing. He filled up the cart and paid for the groceries.

Matt's love and generosity did not stop after the visit to the grocery store. He came back to his office and placed a phone call to a friend who was an athletic trainer at the gym where all TSheets employees received a free membership. Matt scheduled a personal trainer to educate Dave on proper exercise techniques. In addition, Matt contacted another friend to educate and supply Dave with nutritional supplements. The bottom line was that Matt took a personal interest in Dave to help him rebalance.

The time to focus on balance is now. Let's stop competing against our employees' personal drivers. Let's start supporting them and encouraging them to achieve a more balanced lifestyle. They will then put in full, productive, forty-hour weeks. They will be driven to help achieve the company's goals. Remember greater well-being and happiness lead to greater job satisfaction, which leads to increased organizational commitment, a win-win-win for leaders, managers, and employees. And don't forget about the big win at the homes of your employees and managers: families and close relationships will benefit greatly too.

"Quality of time is to quantity of time as actionable love is to thoughts of love."

CHAPTER 2

Family and Friendships: Making Time for Home Life

Which would you rather say on your deathbed: "If only I had spent more time at the office," or "If only I had spent more time with my family and friends"? Most leaders, managers, and employees are too busy running the rat race in corporate America to stop and reflect on what regrets they might have when they face the end of life. I'm sure this is not the first time you've heard the deathbed saying. I remember reading a book that pronounced it is a wise man who learns from his mistakes, yet greater wisdom resides in learning from others' mistakes. I choose to learn from those who wish they had spent more time with their family and close friends.

I wish my friend had thought about spending more time with his brother before he took a phone call that changed his life. He is the former owner of a small business he directed for thirty years. He sold the business and stayed working at the company as the operations manager. He worked a schedule of more than sixty hours per week for the best part of thirty-five years. He worked from 6:30 a.m. to 5:30 p.m., Monday through Friday, and usually, five hours in the morning on Saturdays. He called this his standard workweek. He didn't count the time he worked on the weekends, taking phone calls from his clients.

He carried his cell phone 24/7 in case customers had an issue that needed to be addressed. He was reluctant to turn the phone over to one of his tenured employees because he felt it was his duty to take care of customers. He often complained about being too busy, but he would never let go of even the most remedial daily tasks.

Unfortunately, tragedy struck his family. His brother was rushed to an emergency room and, all of a sudden, my friend was at a hospital bedside with members of his family. The prognosis was gloomy, and time was running out. The family called their parish priest to administer the last rites, a Catholic Christian blessing given near the hour of death. The priest arrived quickly, consoled the family, and began praying over the dying brother. In the middle of the prayer, my friend's phone vibrated. He put his hand on his phone and thought about not answering it. But his loyalty-to-work instinct kicked in. "Hello," he said, as he took the call while walking out of the room. It was from a customer, complaining about some issue. My friend dutifully wrote the information down so he could text message one of his employees to fix the problem. When he returned to the room, his brother had passed.

Tears welled up in his eyes as he told me his story. The moment of holding his brother's hand as he approached death could never be retrieved. Missed moments are exactly that: missed moments. Some are meaningless, but some are tragically costly. Missed moments at the office are meaningless; missed moments with our families and friends can be tragically costly, as my friend discovered.

Today he delegates the on-call duty to the service team. They rotate the weekend responsibility. After this tragedy, my friend changed. He started to prioritize more family events in his life. For example, he now brings his grandson into the office or workshop to share a duty or two together. He is teaching his grandson some of the "tricks of the trade." When the grandson talks about some of the things his knowledgeable grandfather taught him, one can see how proud and happy he is.

This chapter is about prioritizing time with family and close friends as we try to manage the ebbs and flows of our lives. If we don't create time for family and friendship, things will eventually become out of balance. As leaders, we often have the flexibility to adjust our schedules and make accommodations for those we love. We also have the flexibility to adjust our organizational culture to support our managers and employees so they can make time for the loved ones in their lives. Providing more flex-time in their schedules so they too can prioritize family time is a benefit they will cherish. An organization that promotes family time will be rewarded with increased productivity—guaranteed!

Make Time

Every leader, manager, and employee exchanges something for missing moments in the lives of those closest to them. I call this the balance exchange. You should ponder how much your employer pays you to miss your son's or daughter's important game, dance recital, or other family event. You may have had dreams about being involved in your son's or daughter's school activities, sporting or art events. Therefore, I must ask you, "How much is your employer paying you to give up on those dreams? How thick is the guilt laid on you to schedule these important family moments into your work schedule?"

Missing moments with our spouse or significant other has an effect on the balance exchange. You may be considering the effects of being out of town on your anniversary. Anniversaries are about relishing the past, enjoying the present, and making dreams for the future. These moments become memories, and our lives are full of memories. If we don't make time for family and friendships, things go off balance, and we risk missing some crucial moments in our loved ones' lives, especially our children's lives.

Choosing not to make time for family and friendships has negative repercussions in the ebb and flow of our life's balance. We often push our loved ones to the edge and sometimes over it, which can manifest itself as separation, divorce, and disappointed children or friends. All are devastating and wreak havoc in the ebb and flow of balance in the lives of all involved.

The answer to keeping things in balance is choosing to *make time* for them. Yes, it is a choice. It may not seem easy at first, but once you experience the rewards of spending more quality time with your family and friends, you will find it easier to plan and implement.

Time management is key. Consider scheduling lunch with a close friend or family member. If your parents, family, or friends are around and near, perhaps morning coffee with them once a week will be sufficient.

For example, I have been having coffee with my folks for over ten years. I visit them every Wednesday morning. I try to never miss the event. My parents and I have always enjoyed these visits. It's not something that eats up a lot of time, just thirty to forty-five minutes once a week. Remember time is precious for all of us. It is even more precious as we age; it is dear to my parents, who are eighty-two years old. What we do with our time is how we bank our memories. Grab your phone and make a call or send a text message to schedule something with someone you love. Don't be one of those people who are on their deathbed wishing they had spent more time with the people they care about.

Statistics Support Benefits of Family and Friendship Time

Working more than fifty hours a week on a regular basis leads to life-shortening stressors for our mind and bodies. The question to ask yourself is whether you or the people you lead really need to work fifty hours a week to get the job done. Employees and managers are often subject to their own unconscious bias, which directs them to expand their work to fit their given time parameter. This phenomenon, which I discussed earlier, is worth mentioning again. It is known as Parkinson's law: Work expands to fill the time available for its completion. In other words, give people thirty minutes to complete a task and most will take thirty minutes to complete it. Give the same group sixty minutes to complete the exact same task, and many will take sixty minutes to complete it. The duration of the task will expand to fill the time available for its completion.

Many of us, if not all of us, are subject to this unconscious bias. For example, imagine asking an hourly employee to box up some merchandise and ship it out to a customer. We will use the name Lax for this employee. Lax realizes, consciously or subconsciously, there is only one hour left before it is time to clock out for the day. Lax finds himself taking fifteen minutes to find a box for the merchandise, ten minutes to find tape, fifteen minutes to wrap the merchandise in packing material, five minutes to place it in the box, five minutes to tape the box shut, and another ten minutes to print the shipping label and attach it to the box. He was able to expand his work to fill the hour left in the work day. That's Parkinson's law. Lax clocks out with a smile.

Lax has a coworker named Max. The next day, someone asks Max to box up the same kind of merchandise Lax shipped out the previous day. Max is a high-energy person who loves getting things done as quickly as possible. Max spends thirty seconds to locate a box, fifteen seconds to find tape, forty-five seconds to wrap the merchandise in packing material, ten seconds to place it in the box, thirty seconds to tape the box shut, and fifty seconds to print the shipping label and attach it to the box. Max is able to complete Lax's one-hour task in three minutes.

Take a look around your workplace to see if you can identify Parkinson's law at play. This old saying really is true: if you need to delegate something to get it done, give it to a busy person.

Although hourly, nonexempt employees are guaranteed overtime compensation for working more than forty hours per week, many of our managers and leaders are the ones working more than fifty hours. In addition, the US workforce has many fewer manufacturing workers than it had many decades ago. Today's workforce consists more of workers with specialized skills and knowledge. The employees in this new generation are known as knowledge workers. They are, typically, exempt from having to follow the standard forty-hour workweek. It is expected and demanded by many employers that our knowledge workers and managers work more than fifty hours each week—without overtime pay. It may well be time for our culture to reflect on the reasons for the forty-hour standard.

Have you ever wondered how the forty-hour workweek originated? It has been the US standard for over seventy-five years. Many factors, such as accidents in the workplace and a culmination of workplace developments helped this standard become law in 1940.

The eight-hour workday became very popular when the Ford Motor Company scaled back from forty-eight hours to forty hours in 1914. Henry Ford made a bold move. He increased the daily pay from $2.34 per nine-hour workday to $5 per eight-hour workday. He more than doubled the wage, removed eight hours from the workweek, and increased the overall output of his workforce. Yes, people became more productive when working eight fewer hours per week.

In a 1922 *New York Times* article, Edsel Ford, Henry's son, stated, "The Ford Company always has sought to promote an ideal home life for its employees. We believe that in order to live properly every man should have more time to spend with his family." More time with family, coupled with a fair wage and working conditions, improved productivity nearly one-hundred years ago.

Today's leaders can learn from Edsel Ford's brilliant decision and from other countries around the world that have improved productivity while providing employees and managers more time with their family and friends. For example, Germans, on average, work about 1,436 hours per year, as opposed to the 1,804 hours Americans work. Meanwhile, studies show that Germans get roughly the same amount of work done in fewer hours each week and with more vacation time.

Baby Boomers Need a Paradigm Shift

More hours worked at the office or shop does not mean more output. More output means more output. Boomers have worked and lived under the premise that working very long hours and weekends shows they care about the company and are loyal. In some boomers' eyes, it means they are top producers and the most valuable employees and managers of the company. I encourage boomers and some Generation Xers to begin looking through a different lens. A millennial's perspective shows more output can be achieved by embracing the needs of employees and managers. Millennials and some Xers have learned that embracing technology has given them the ability to produce more in fewer hours than many of their coworkers.

However, our three-generational workforce comes with its challenges. For instance, I have a millennial friend who is a long-term substitute teacher in an inner-city public school district. She gets paid for seven and a half hours of work per day at a rate equivalent to some cities' minimum wage. The Generation X principal of the school suggested to her that she work longer hours at the school. The principal told my friend that staying after school would serve as an example to other teachers because working late would prove she "truly" cared about her students. My millennial friend told her principal, "I have a master's degree in mathematics. My students are falling in love with math for the first time in their lives. I use the technology we have in the classroom and have my students participate in creating and building our lesson plans. It is part of their learning process. I don't need to stay after school and pretend I have additional work to do for the sake of others seeing me there. The results of my students' attitudes about math and their test scores speak for my methods. After school is my time to meet up with friends or visit the gym." I hope the principal learns to appreciate this millennial's perspective and methods for achieving output and balance in life.

Tactics to Restore More Family Time

BREAKING BREAD

I grew up in an era of communal meals. I was the youngest of six children. Dinner, or as we called it, supper, was at 6:00 p.m., seven days per week. My dad worked until 5:30 p.m., and my mom always cooked for the family. We ate out twice a year during the Christmas season. Eating at the kitchen table and talking about our day's events was the way our family communicated with each other. If one of us could not make it to supper, my mom would make a plate of food, wrap it in aluminum foil, and place it in the oven to keep warm. When family members arrived home from football, baseball, track, or drill team practice, my mom, and usually a sister, would sit with them while they ate their supper. I have many great memories of family discussions at the kitchen table. Some people may think of this as old fashioned, too conservative, and not applicable today. I say it's about as old fashioned and conservative as freedom in America. We are not willing to give up our freedoms. Therefore, we should not be willing to give up on family traditions.

When I became an adult, I brought the family dinner concept to my own family and carried on the tradition. I find it one of the greatest meeting and communication centers in the house. I added my own flare to the mix. I enjoy cooking with my wife immensely, and once in a while one of the kids will join in, especially if that kid sees a box of brownies in the pantry. When my wife and I prepare the meal, we usually also enjoy a nice glass of wine together. The kids sometimes join the kitchen festivities. However, in today's world, getting everyone together is challenging. If you don't have time to cook, you could order a pizza and gather the family around the kitchen table so you can all inquire about each other's day. Take time to actively listen to family members and respond. I encourage all of you to avoid having the TV on or having your cell phones available during this dinner time. Remember a great technique for cell phone addiction is to place phones in the middle of the table and take a short retreat from connectivity.

COUCH TIME

When each of my children turned about three years old, I would sit them on one side of the couch and I would take the other. We turned to face each other, often dangling our feet over each other's legs. The room was filled with silence. The other family members were busy doing something. TV, music, and smartphones were absent. We simply sat in silence, and I would start the conversation with something such as, "So, tell me about what you did today." Family members would tell me all kinds of things they did that day. I often asked probing questions to expand the conversation. We usually spent only about fifteen minutes on the couch while they talked about their day, and then I would share a little bit about mine. This became beneficial during the preteen and teen years. As my children grew, they began to ask me about my day, which I found very rewarding. This venue of communication became a tradition my children and I looked forward to every week.

As children grow older, there may be less couch time due to busy schedules, but when you are committed to building relationships with your children, capitalizing on impromptu discussions is worth pursuing. Couch time may be accomplished in different ways. For instance, when I drive my kids to school or sports practice, I try to use that time to talk with them. I found turning off the radio helps, but jamming on classic rock music can show the kids we parents are human too.

Couch time for our older children may come via phone or video. My oldest daughter is in college, and she often calls me on Sunday evenings to talk about her week. She asks me about my week, and as we progress through the conversation, I am often reminded of the many times we sat on the couch, doing the same thing. When times get stressful in my family, I am reminded of the many benefits of couch time, and I usually circle back and spend more one-on-one time with my children—often on the couch.

DATE NIGHT

I have found that one-on-one dates are a great way to build relationships. I used to have date nights with my children when they were young. I would often take them to a restaurant for dessert. Since I have four children, I could only do this about once every couple of weeks with each child. We have many great memories of these dates. Today our dates have changed from desserts to coffee cafés. The venue doesn't really matter; it's the one-on-one time that counts.

As I mentioned earlier in the book, I remarried. I did not include my first wife in my relationship dating practice. Our relationship never grew; it simply grew apart. We focused on the children as a means to avoid the reality that we did not get along very well. My wife and I today enjoy our date nights immensely. We reserve Tuesday nights for our date night, and nothing is allowed to get in the way of our going to dinner, indulging in a glass of wine, and enjoying each other's company. We have been doing this for over three years, which has helped our relationship grow in a positive and rewarding manner.

How to Find the Time

Even if it's hard, you find the time by *making* time for your family and friendships. When my two youngest girls were in competitive gymnastics, they would be at the gym training from 4:00 p.m. to 8:00 p.m., three nights per week. They would get a twenty-minute snack break around 6:00 p.m. I found myself showing up between 5:30 and 5:45 p.m. each night so I could watch them practice for a few minutes. When the team took their snack break, my girls would join me in the bleachers and eat. I would take this time to ask them about their day and to share a little bit about mine. I did this three nights a week for three years. I simply ended my day at the office and made sure I could make it from work to the gym on time. I will restate part of what I just said: I simply ended my day! Yes, you too have more control over your day and schedule than you may think. **Prioritize, negotiate, and do whatever you need to do to make the time for your family and yourself.** The rewards are tremendous. One year at the annual awards banquet, the coaches created and presented me with the Snack Daddy of the Year award. They thanked me for my dedication to being an involved father. To this day, it is one of the greatest awards I have received. My girls still talk about how I was such of a big part of their gymnastics experience.

As stated previously, I text and frequently talk on the phone with my daughter in college. We usually chat on Sundays and after I teach at the university on Tuesday evenings. She likes to hear about my lectures and how I get the students to participate. I learned over the years that I need to be more giving with my life, meaning I need to allow others into my world and share with them my highs, lows, and all points in between. I demonstrate this by not only asking my daughter how she is doing in college but also by sharing the high-lights of my day or week. It takes practice. I am not a natural conver-sationalist, especially when talking about myself. I encourage you to reach out to members of your family or friendship group and start sharing more of yourself with them.

I know it can be easier said than done when it comes to building a more communicative relationship with a child, spouse, or friend. There are ebbs and flows in the communication challenges I have with various people. During the past several years, my challenge to effectively reach my son and have meaningful conversations with him met many hurdles. I think those of you who have teenagers will know what I mean. After many attempts to bring us closer, I knew I had to wait for him to reach out to me. It finally came when he asked for my help with enlisting in the army. I was with him for all twelve meetings, the swearing-in ceremony, and his pre-enlistment training. I am extremely proud of him for finding something meaningful and making long-term plans for a career. Sometimes, finding or making the time is about putting yourself in a position to rise to the occasion when family and friends reach out to you. It is about the ebb and flow of balance in your life. It is about putting forth the energy where your energy is needed.

On the other hand, finding time to keep life in balance over a period of time is challenging. The career elements in my life consist of consulting, speaking, teaching, doctorate studies, research, and writing. I find success in making time for my family by "pausing" my working day by 5:00 p.m. or 5:30 p.m. We try to have dinner together. However, I find myself picking up kids from practice or going to their games once or twice a week. When we are all together in the early evening, I usually find myself sitting at the dining room table placing myself in the presence of one or more of my children doing homework. It is a great time for me to be with my children and gives me a chance to participate in an activity with them: homework. I take this opportunity to share my schoolwork and research. When my children finish their work, I put my projects down too. I try to spend thirty minutes of free time with them before I switch the focus of my energy to my wife. She and I try to dedicate an hour of time with each other. It may not sound like much, but if you put down the smartphones and laptops, turn off the TV, turn toward each other, and talk, that hour is one of the most relaxing and enjoyable moments of the day.

Vacation is another area where I try to manage my time. Many of us are needed back at the office or by a client. I make time for these work-related activities by rising early in the morning before the family awakes. It is quiet and peaceful, and it allows me to work with a focus. I attempt to accomplish everything I need to do in the morning so I can focus on my family when I am with them later in the day. Vacation should center on having fun and spending meaningful time with your family. Family time should rise to the pinnacle of the ebb and flow balance chart.

Time for Self

We must not forget to make time for ourselves. Spending time engaged in a hobby or something that we thoroughly enjoy is required for sustained happiness, according to most positive psychologists. In writing this section of the chapter, I spent time reflecting on what I have done over the years to make time for myself. I realized I had been doing a good job at making time for others, yet not for myself. Some may say I make time to exercise and spend time with family. However, no one has ever accused me of being selfish with my time and only doing something just for myself. I recognized that I was out of balance. I checked this thought with a few loved ones, and they concurred. I am missing the "self-time" in my life, something I can get excited about and engaged in, something that makes me oblivious to the passing of time. I need to find something I have fun doing for the sake of doing it, not because it is productive or will improve something in my life. Where do I begin?

Gretchen Rubin, author of the New York Times best seller *The Happiness Project*, suggests we begin by thinking about things we enjoyed doing for fun as children. For me, it was building model cars and helping my parents in their small garden. Over the years, I have grown tomato plants and other vegetables on a part-time basis. This means I did not spend much time gardening. I just tried to get the fruits off the vine. I have pondered my lack of "self-time" and discovered I actually do enjoy gardening, yet I have never allowed myself to take the self-time needed to produce a fun and rewarding garden.

I am happy to say I have started making plans to incorporate self-time into my schedule and dedicate it to preparing a garden. My tasks begin with getting the seeds of many different vegetables. Much of the planning and work may be dedicated to self-time, but there will be ample opportunity to have my children and wife join in on the fun once in a while. It will be another way for us to spend quality time together as a family. And, of course, the fruits of our labor will become the ingredients we use to prepare family meals as we spend time cooking together.

Technology Can Find Time for You

You can use technology to monitor your technology. In other words, what sometimes keeps us from spending time with our family can help us reunite. Ironically, the thing that sometimes takes up a lot of our time is the thing that can get us back in balance!

It may be helpful to track how many minutes you spend on your phone all day. Moment is an application that can help you. You may be surprised at how much time you give to your smartphone. If others complain to you about how often you check your phone, then Checky may be an app for you to investigate. It tracks how frequently you check your phone. My favorite app is Offtime. This application informs others that you are unplugged from 24/7/365 connectivity to take a well-deserved break. You can find all three of these apps in the app store.

SINGLE PARENT TACTICS FOR MORE TIME

Being a single parent is especially hard. One important fact to remember is that it is about the *quality* of time spent, not the *amount* of time. You don't need to beat yourself up with guilt. However, we often make ourselves feel guilty, which leads to spending more time with our children while we are deepening our stressors due to worry or lack of sleep. An alternative approach is to focus on being engaged with your child. You can do this in many ways. It could be leading an informative conversation in the car ride to school or preparing and eating dinner together at home. Shorter, less frequent, but intensely engaged energy with your child is what most current studies suggest as a tactic to parent effectively. In order to do this, you need to free yourself of "time quantity" guilt trips and allow yourself to focus on the "now," whether that is work, exercise, meeting a friend, or being engaged with your child.

When my wife was a single parent, she found taking an interest in her children's activities often provided topics to discuss with them. For instance, if her child was reading a popular book series, she would pick up an extra copy at the library and read it too. She found talking to her children about a book she was reading provided them with meaningful discussion. Once the movie came out about the book, they were first in line to enjoy another few hours of quality time.

A method we both employed, as parents, was to make the best use of time when we were taking our children to their football or soccer practice. I would take my son to his football practice four nights per week. The practices would usually last about one and a half hours. I would take the first forty-five minutes to run around the park where the practice was being held before watching him practice for the remainder of the session. I achieved two goals: exercising to help me stay physically and mentally fit and engagement in an activity that my child enjoyed. My wife also used her child's practice time in a positive and beneficial manner. She would engage in friendship time with some of the other soccer moms. Grown-up girl time has always been and continues to be important to her. She found soccer practice to be an event where she could spend time with girlfriends while engaging in one of her child's interests.

Value of Friendship

Married people say friendship is more than five times as important as physical intimacy in the marriage, according to Tom Rath, author of *Vital Friends: The People You Can't Afford to Live Without*. I do not see friendship and physical intimacy with my spouse as mutually exclusive. Rather, I see them as interdependent: the greater the friendship, the greater the intimacy. Friendship is like many other important things in life: it requires attention and energy. For instance, because my wife has a need to talk through her problems, she needs me to listen and listen and then listen some more. Listening to five renditions of the same problem requires patience, love, energy, and understanding. She was gracious enough to teach me that she is not looking for me to solve her problem; she just wants me to understand and have empathy. She generally has the problem under control, but she has a need to discuss it at some length because that is one way she wants to bond with me. When I finally learned to listen by showing understanding and empathy, I was able to deepen our friendship and relationship.

Being friends with our spouse, significant other, or our children is great but insufficient. We spend more waking hours of our lives at work than we do in our special relationships. According to Tom Rath, those who say they have no real friends at work have only an 8 percent chance of feeling engaged in their job. Conversely, having a "best friend at work" makes employees seven times more likely to feel engaged in their job. According to positive psychologist and author Martin Seligman, engagement in work is one of the five components of happiness. Having a few great friendships is another one of the five elements for sustained happiness.

Finding Time for Friends

I must follow the advice of my wife because I am a beginner at finding and making time for friends. You see, I have not been one of those guys, husbands, or dads who put friends in front of family when it comes to prioritizing time. I am actually one of those guys who did not develop many friends outside a close circle of people I work with. Reflecting on my career, I regret not including friends in my balance of life. As a matter of fact, the original title of this chapter was "Family." The title changed to "Family and Friendships," thanks to a student of mine named David. In reviewing the concept for my book, he told me he considered his friends as family and encouraged me to include the word *friendships* in the chapter title. Not only did he open my mind to the importance of friends, but he also helped me discover that my limited circle of friends was causing imbalance in my life. My wife, Marlene, is my relationship coach. Her best friend is her mom. She talks to her every day on her drive to work. (She is a schoolteacher.) After work, she frequently stops to visit her mom and dad for an hour or so. Marlene and her mom thoroughly enjoy their time together. They watch TV shows, go to lunch together, watch movies, shop, shop some more, and so on.

Marlene takes this mother-daughter friendship model and applies it to her girlfriends too. She makes time for a friend or two every week. They love to get together for happy hour at a restaurant, visit and talk for an hour or two, and repeat the experience every other week. Sometimes one of them has the others over to her home to cook dinner together and have girl time.

She has been coaching me on reaching out to old friends I have neglected over the years. She knows I enjoy their company and the camaraderie of guy time. She also knows I have an extremely high propensity to put my children or her in front of friendship time. She helps me combat my natural tendency by encouraging me to schedule an activity with a friend. It could mean meeting up with a buddy for a cup of java at our favorite coffee house. Or we may find ourselves at one of the local brew pubs enjoying one or two latest craft beer offerings.

Balancing Family and Friendship

Finding time for both family and friends can be a challenge because you don't want to go too far in any direction. As you have read, I spent years and years focusing my time on family and was completely out of balance regarding friendships. It has been important for me to realize that developing meaningful friendships requires energy and time, the same elements involved in fostering family relationships.

One could say I am a practicing friendship developer. The first part of this practice consists of being observant of my environment. For example, the other day, I was invited to lunch via a text message from a friend I had made during a cooperative business arrangement. In other words, we did some business consulting for the same client and developed an appreciation for each other's work. I wanted to meet up with him for a beer or two, but my schedule was too busy. At least, that is what I told myself when I told him I wanted to meet up but couldn't do it that week. When I shared this information with my relationship coach, she encouraged me to text him and arrange my schedule to accommodate our meeting. As she so graciously engrained in me, "This invite may not be about you; he may need your help and is seeking you out for friendship." I followed her advice and have been thankful ever since. I have developed a great friendship in which we have fun and rewarding conversation. We often bounce ideas and problems off each other and exchange objective, nonjudgmental opinions to help solve problems.

The spirit of this book is about balancing the ebbs and flows of daily demands. While I have neglected friendships in my past and have learned how to correct my imbalance, others may find themselves choosing friends over family. I notice this once in a while at the golf course. I am not an avid golfer, but I do enjoy getting out on the green on a beautiful sunny day. When I decide to play a round of golf, it is during the week, and I will finish before the business day is over. Every now and then, I hear people scheduling their next rounds of play. Oftentimes their schedule includes a Saturday or Sunday. I know many of these folks already work long hours, and I am surprised they choose to take more time with friends from work on days that many of us devote to family time. Please remember it's about balance. Playing golf or another activity on the weekend every now and then is healthy. However, taking time away from the family every weekend in the summer may cause unhealthy stress that can produce major family complications.

Leadership at Work

As a leader in your organization, family time and friendships are important for your team members and employees. Many leaders understand the natural competition organizations and employees engage in with each other. The leader often makes the organization's goals the priority, while employees and managers, although they respect and work toward their organizational goals, also strive for their personal goals in life. Natural competition is prevalent in every organization. Individuals' goals may include more time with family, exercise, or just downtime. Work-life balance is different for everyone. Remember, too much time at the office leads to low productivity. Competing with your employees and managers by not truly understanding them as individuals also leads to low productivity. Pushing them to such an extent that they are in competition with their own individual goals will cause trouble. If employees become resentful because they cannot make time for their family, they will not perform well, burn out, and eventually, leave. If you are really unlucky, they will quit but continue to show up every day to collect a paycheck.

Alex, one of my university students, told me that having a work-life balance means having an employer whom he can trust when he explains he is going through a hard time in his personal life and could use a slightly lighter workload for a few days. "It's really very simple," Alex said. "Please recognize me as a human being and treat me as such." When personal issues come up, employees should not feel they are cheating their employer by addressing their personal needs or family's needs.

A leadership practice I implemented many years ago consisted of insisting that my managers and employees leave work early to see their children play a game or attend a dance, art show, or other event. It was and is important for me to have all members of the organization spend time attending their family events. If leaders support their employees in this type of endeavor, positive emotions and organizational engagement will increase. Their employees will be more likely to achieve their work objectives with positive emotion and engagement and be happier, balanced, and more fulfilled at work and at home.

I used to work for a very supportive CEO. His name was Vince, and he was very loyal to everyone who worked with him. He called us family. He taught us that respecting individuals and their families was a duty, an honor, and a privilege. I believe his service to our country in the US Marine Corps helped shape his leadership beliefs. He always walked the talk and led by example.

"Hey, Donnie, today is your last day in the office before you take your family on vacation isn't it," Vince once asked me.

"Yes, it is! I'm just finishing up the reports I promised you and will be heading out soon," I said.

"That's great," Vince replied. "Oh, by the way, here's a little something for your vacation." He pulled a hundred dollar bill out of his desk drawer and poured us a splash of Scotch. "This is for you. I want you to take your family out to dinner. I want them to know how much I appreciate your contributions to our success and how much I appreciate you as an individual and as a family person," he said. "Now, raise your glass. Let's toast to a happy and safe time for you and your family. Salut." We nodded at each other and downed the Scotch.

Vince gave me a hundred dollars every year before our summer vacation. After the first time he gave it to me, he said, "Now go and do the same for your management team and employees." I had a staff of six managers and forty-five employees. I followed Vince's lead. It is a tradition I continue to implement within my small company and one that I advocate to my clients.

Reflection Activity for Individuals

Often, we are so busy that we skip the opportunity to communicate constructively with ourselves. Learning journals can help you stretch yourself, push the boundaries of your thinking, pose questions, and make meaning out of your work experiences and relationships. Start taking a look at how much time you devote to your family life and friendships and where you could be making some changes to get more in balance. Jotting some notes down in a journal or on your computer could be a great way to begin. If you are someone who likes to write in the book you are reading, please add your notes in the following box.

REFLECTION BOX

Write a note to yourself in this box, briefly describing how you could make some changes so you can spend more time with your family and friends.

Reflection Activity for Managers

Take a look at how much time you allot for your employees to devote to their family time. Take an inventory of your employees' personal information including their spouse's name, number of children, ages, family activities such as soccer, football, dance, and so on. Add to your learning journal the information you gather about your employees. The following table provides an example of the information that would be helpful to make informed decisions on how to best serve your employees.

Employee & Dept.	Spouse	Children & Age	Family or Employee Activities	Season, Day, and Time of Activities	Employee's Needs
James A. Production	Maria	Danielle, 13 Thomas, 10	Soccer Basketball	Spring: Wed. 4:00 p.m. Winter: Tues 5:00 p.m.	Leave work by 3:30 p.m. on Wed. Leave work by 4:30 p.m. on Tues.
Mindy Z.	N/A	N/A	Exercise Class	All: M, W, F 6:30 a.m. - 7:30 a.m.	Shift start time from 8:00 a.m. to 8:30 a.m.

REFLECTION BOX

What can you do, as a leader in your organization, to help your managers and employees attend their children's events such as sports, dance recitals, or other activities?

"The greatest prescription for healthy living is active prevention."

CHAPTER 3

Good Health: Making Time to Exercise and Eat Well

The latest research states that nearly 100 percent of Fortune 500 CEOs are in excellent shape from diet and exercise and have a good body mass index (BMI) rating. *The Wall Street Journal* produced an article about BMI and how one's fit appearance produces a perception of leadership ability and effectiveness. Whether we wish to be a leader in an organization, our families, our communities or a CEO of a publically traded company, the benefits to us and everyone associated with us are greatly influenced by our good or poor health habits.

As many of you know, when you eat healthy food and exercise regularly, you are physically, mentally, and emotionally stronger. These benefits manifest themselves in many ways, such as having more energy at work and home, having the ability to mentally focus on specific tasks, and being emotionally balanced to manage the stresses of life. Yet only one-third of the American adult population appears to be successfully practicing good daily health habits.

This chapter is about prioritizing healthy eating and exercise habits when we try to prioritize the ebbs and flows of our lives. If we don't create time for healthy eating and exercising, things will eventually slip out of balance. We can, sometimes, drop the ball with family, faith, and career, but when we drop the ball because we aren't eating healthy food and exercising, we may drop dead. All other areas of our lives are recoverable and forgivable, but our health does not always follow suit. As leaders, we often have the flexibility to adjust our schedules to fit in an exercise program. We also have the flexibility to adjust our organizational culture to support our managers and employees so they too can make time for eating healthy food and exercising. Providing more flex-time in their schedules for this purpose will not only improve their lives but bring greater productivity to our organization. Leaders who promote eating healthy food and exercising will be rewarded with increased productivity—guaranteed!

One-Third, One-Third, and One-Third

It's hard to believe that in America over one-third of adults are obese, one-third are overweight, and only one-third are within the healthy range, according to the US Department of Health and Human Services. The latest figure from my research says 75 percent of men are overweight or obese. People may be spending too much time putting in hours at the office while not spending any time on healthy self-care habits resulting in an imbalanced life. They suffer from type 2 diabetes, cardiovascular disease, depression, and many other debilitating diseases. According to the Centers of Disease Control and Prevention, the majority of them die prematurely due to this imbalance.

Serious Repercussions

One of my best friends is more than ninety pounds overweight. I have asked him the same question for over ten years. "Do you wish to start exercising and stop eating donuts before or after your heart attack?" Though my question to my friend may sound harsh and insensitive to his feelings, I have been trying to get him to change his health habits because of the love I have for him.

My friend Bruce is a great guy. He will do anything for anyone. He is a true gentlemen and Christian. He is married to the love of his life and has three children. Bruce is the guy who spends an enormous amount of time serving his family, friends, and coworkers. He is a giver. He commutes to work for more than an hour, sits at a desk for ten hours writing computer code, and tries to find time to meet me for a cup of java on his way home once a week.

I have, literally, asked Bruce the question about his health hundreds and hundreds of times. You see, Bruce is fifty-five years old. His father passed away from a heart attack at age fifty-eight. His grandfather passed away from a heart attack at fifty-six. Bruce is approaching the odds, but they are not odds I'd like him to gamble on. He has a son who recently married, a daughter in medical school, and another daughter getting ready to graduate from high school. His lovely wife is a nurse at the local hospital.

Perhaps you know of someone like Bruce, or perhaps you are that person. Making the time to exercise and eat well needs to begin now. We need to reverse the trend of poor health and lose weight to get healthier now, not tomorrow. I am reminded of the Chinese proverb: When is the best time to plant a tree? "Fifty years ago," the wise person says. And the second-best time is now.

Another friend of mine, Charlie, planted his tree of healthy habits four years ago. He lost seventy-five pounds in eighteen months. He successfully changed his dietary habits, began a basic exercise program, and stuck with the changes until his new habits were on auto pilot.

I asked Charlie, "How did you do it? How did you finally decide to make a change?"

Charlie said, "I went to a new doctor for my annual physical. My doctor told me, don't make any changes, and you will die prematurely. Lose seventy-five pounds, and you will live a healthy and happier life. If you lose the weight and continue to eat a balanced diet and exercise, you will live to enjoy your grandchildren one day."

Do you need to plant your tree? Do you know of anyone whose time is now to plant the tree of healthy living? Bruce, plant your tree!

Benefits of Good Health Habits

EATING

Let's not kid ourselves. We eat too much of the wrong foods and not enough natural foods such as fruits, vegetables, grains, and nuts. We have developed a culture of believing bigger and more is always better. McDonald's perfected the famous sales pitch of "Would you like fries with that?" and followed it with "Would you like to supersize that order for fifty cents more?" After all, it's only fifty cents.

Whether you are an executive, midlevel manager, or an employee working in the office or on the production line, maintaining a balanced diet is challenging. Before you know it, you are pushing to get to the office early, preparing for a client meeting, and working late to meet a deadline. Breakfast was a cup of java, lunch was eating a bagel in the car, and dinner was an all-you-can-eat refrigerator raid or a four-thousand-calorie dinner at the restaurant.

It all starts with breakfast. Now, I know you heard your parents tell you that breakfast is the most important meal of the day. The reason for this is because it ends your brain's fast from glucose during your night's sleep. Glucose is one of the brain's primary sources of energy, and it does not have a built-in storage reserve. Science has proven that eating breakfast will improve your attitude and increase concentration and problem-solving abilities. Therefore, start eating something in the morning before you head off to work. Your brain will thank you by responding with a sense of well-being through the early part of the day. Next up: don't neglect your lunch.

There are many studies that have successfully demonstrated a cause-and-effect relationship between what we eat for lunch and productivity in the workplace. Ideally, we should try to maintain a steady blood sugar level throughout the day. Just about everything we eat turns into glucose, which affords the energy our brain needs to concentrate and stay active. Our bodies break down the foods we consume into glucose, but not all foods get broken down at the same rate. If we eat a simple carbohydrate meal of pasta, breads, and sugars, we will get a burst of energy, followed by a sluggish period for the rest of the day, which lowers productivity. If we consume a burger and fries for lunch, our digestive system has to work harder, which reduces the oxygen levels in our brain. A reduction of oxygen in the brain also gives us the groggy feeling that lowers our productivity.

Planning what we will eat for lunch ensures we eat foods high in protein and complex carbohydrates. A salad with chicken is an example of this type of meal. I recommend staying away from bread, which is my Achilles heel. It guarantees my afternoon will only be one-third as productive as it can and should be.

Although this book is not a diet book, I do have another interesting food study to share. The *British Journal of Health Psychology* has featured numerous articles on how eating up to seven servings per day of fruits and vegetables has a positive effect on our cognitive and emotional well-being. Several studies concluded people who eat more fruits and vegetables are happier, more engaged in their work or other activities, and more creative in problem solving. The science behind the study suggests people receive vital nutrients from these foods that promote the brain's production of dopamine. Dopamine is a neurotransmitter that makes us feel more curious, motivated, and engaged. Fruits and vegetables also provide a valuable supply of antioxidants that help reduce inflammation, improve memory, and enhance our mood with positive emotions.

EXERCISE

I begin by saying there are studies that say exercising just twenty minutes a day can help substantially in the long run—for example, by cutting the risk of premature death by one-third. However, exercising for forty minutes to work up a good sweat will help you significantly reduce your stress while providing all of the cardiovascular benefits. With forty minutes of exercise and twenty minutes to get yourself cleaned up, you have it all accomplished in one hour.

Study after study reveals exercising on a regular basis will improve concentration and memory, promote faster learning, enhance creativity, and lower your stress. Believe me, I agree with these studies 100 percent. For example, on days when I'm preparing one of my university lectures or class discussions, I often have to take a break to pound the pavement with a three-mile run. I come back to my lesson plan and fill in all of the gaps. I can do this easily because I can concentrate significantly better while enjoying a sense of calmness throughout my mind and body.

When it comes to eating healthy food and exercising, we should do what the CEOs do in Fortune 500 companies. A majority of them include eating well and exercising as part of their routine.

They actually consider it a part of their job. They do this because they experience an overpowering sense of wellness, well-being, and calmness throughout their day. It helps them think more clearly and more strategically, with an understanding that they are in control.

SLEEP

Eating well and exercising regularly are two-thirds of the equation of good health. We must also remember to get enough sleep and understand the importance of it. This is the area that seems to go out of balance for me. When the ebb and flow of balance is disrupted, getting adequate rest is one of the first things to go. Over the years, I have learned that pushing myself too hard will result in my getting a cold or some other seasonal illness. I have realized through trial and error the importance of listening to my mind and body when it tells me it needs rest.

We are all more productive and better in the long run when we receive the proper amount of sleep. The downside of not getting enough sleep includes low productivity, moodiness, anxiety, lack of clarity in thought, weight gain, and disease. None of these outcomes sound attractive. Therefore, if we are going to exercise and eat a well-rounded, healthy diet, we must ensure we get adequate sleep so we can receive all of the health benefits.

REDUCING STRESS

We know if we eat more fruits and vegetables, followed by a daily exercise regimen, and get adequate rest, we will be in a great position to fight off stress. Our body and mind will naturally manage hurtful stress and turn it into a positive stress that keeps us motivated to perform, yet does not bury us with cognitive or emotional overload.

A very common, yet unhealthy way of attempting to reduce stress is excessive alcohol drinking and binge eating. This practice leads to increasing the imbalance in our lives and promotes obesity, family problems, and possibly, career problems.

The underlying premise of this book is managing balance. Binging and overindulging destroy balance. Whether it is binging with alcohol, food, work, family time, or worship, too much of a good thing results in it becoming a detractor to balance. Enjoying an adult beverage or two may provide positive effects to your balance. Throwing back a six-pack of beer, followed by binge eating before you go to bed leads to imbalance. Moderation is the key to successfully balancing our life and living a successful and rewarding life.

Tactics to Add and Maintain Good Health Habits

In the previous chapter, I talked about the family cooking together as a way to spend quality time together. Cooking together brings with it the added benefit of eating a healthy and balanced diet. I thoroughly enjoy cooking with my wife or one or more of my children. Though we don't always make the healthiest meals, it does give us a chance to include healthy items in our meals. Remember, balance is the key.

We need to exercise regularly. There is no magic pill that can take the place of exercise. Some of you reading this book already exercise as a part of your daily routine. Stick with it! Some of you used to exercise until your life got too busy. Perhaps the reason was marriage, children, or a new career.

I want you to find something active to do and do it now. Go ahead and put this book down and go for a twenty-minute walk. The time to start an exercise lifestyle is now. You may have something that you really enjoy doing but have not done for a long time. It could be tennis, swimming, running, dancing, walking the golf course, walking the dog, or weight training. Whatever it is, find something you love doing and make it a part of your routine, even if it is only for twenty minutes. Allow yourself to exercise and begin to feel an increase in energy, focus, emotional balance, and well-being.

We want to manage our stress successfully by eating healthier food, exercising, and getting adequate rest. For some of us, it may mean getting eight hours of sleep, for others it may be less than eight. Regardless of the number, be sure you understand how much sleep your mind and body require. When you feel overly stressed or are having trouble focusing clearly, get up from your chair and do your twenty-minute walk. If you want to accelerate the stress management process, begin praying or meditating during your walk. The exercise and mental imagery will bring clarity to your thoughts once you return to your work environment.

Using your time wisely during the day is fundamental to a successful balance. If you find yourself eating at your desk while you try to get caught up on your work, you will find yourself out of balance. Taking time away from your daily grind is an important element in stress management. Perhaps you could walk to a local eatery and dine with a friend from work. Other days, you could choose to bring your lunch to work and walk to a pretty area to eat. Getting away from the daily grind, exercising your body and mind with a walk, and fueling your body with high protein and complex carbohydrates is a proven formula for being more productive and happy at work.

Those of you who say walking at lunchtime is not enough should incorporate your favorite exercise into your schedule before or after work. I love starting my day with a three-mile run. I get to enjoy the outdoors and have the time to contemplate what I desire to achieve for that day. Running allows me time to put things into perspective.

I try to use that time to step back from my daily grind and make sure I am working on the things that are important in my life.

Manufacturing New Habits

I use the word *manufacturing* because I and others believe we can systematically manufacture new habits if we understand the build process. The author and Harvard psychologist Shawn Achor explains how developing a new habit is all about removing the obstacles that prevent us from performing a task or changing our behavior. In his book *The Happiness Advantage*, Shawn Achor discusses how we can systematically remove obstacles. He uses the example of getting up in the morning and going for a run. When we wake to the alarm clock and begin to think consciously about going for our morning run, we immediately shift our thoughts to what we need to do in order to execute this desired behavior. First, we think about where our running shorts, shirt, socks, and shoes are located. My shoes may be in the garage or front closet. We may ask ourselves if we have any clean running socks to wear. Essentially, we allow our mental abilities to place "obstacles" in our way from executing our desired behavior. Shawn Achor talks about what he calls the twenty-second rule. If we can get engaged with the desired behavior (new habit) in less than twenty seconds, we have a much greater chance of developing the new habit over a period of time. Achor suggests, as many psychologists do, we have to do something at least twenty-one times for our new habit to be sustainable.

If I wake up in the morning intending to go on a morning run or head to the gym and have to think about where to find my exercise clothes and shoes, I've probably already used up more than twenty seconds. Running around the house gathering these items takes up several minutes even for the most organized persons among us.

Achor, who had trouble building the morning run habit, decided he needed to take serious measures to remove his obstacles. He began to sleep in his running clothes and socks. He placed his shoes on the side of his bed the night before his run. When the alarm clock woke him up in the morning, he simply slipped his running shoes on and headed for the door. He did this more than twenty-one times, and a new habit of running was established.

You may wish to begin walking during your lunch break at the office. I know many people who say they would like to walk, but their walking shoes are at home. These folks could bring their shoes to the office and place them under their desk so they can be slipped on at lunchtime. You won't have time to think of reasons why you can't walk; you will be too busy heading out the door in your walking shoes. By the way, take the shoes off and place them back under your desk so they are there the next day. No need to make yourself remember to bring them every day.

Sustainability Is Key

Just as we wish for our new habits to have a long shelf life, we should pause and reflect on some of our current habits to ensure they are sustainable and valuable for the long run. For instance, though alcohol is okay for most people, stress can cause us to overdo it. Coffee is fine but not when we're constantly chugging it to stay energized. The point is to not overdo it. The key is balance, which will ensure that it is sustainable.

Many years ago, I was listening to a program that explained how meat is produced. It was a horrible description, and I stopped eating meat that day. After one week of becoming a vegetarian, I noticed all of my neck pain and tightness was gone. I had suffered from periodic neck pain for decades and could not have been more ecstatic about my pain disappearing.

Over the course of a year or two, I found myself craving certain meat items. I felt as if I were missing some vitamins or nutrients even though I was taking vitamin supplements. I began to experiment with taking a bite or two of meat, usually from the plate of one of my children. It took me a year to pinpoint the problem. I was allergic to the proteins in beef. I noticed during my experimental year that taking a bite or two of a cheeseburger caused inflammation to occur in my body within hours. My neck regained its former pain and stiffness. After about thirty-six hours, it subsided. I experimented with chicken, pork, and seafood. Nothing else caused the pain to come back. It was at this moment that I began balancing my diet with chicken, pork, and seafood. I have remained on this balanced diet ever since I discovered beef caused inflammation in me. Being a complete vegetarian was difficult to sustain. Eating just about anything I want except for beef is much more sustainable for me. Balance is key. Too much or too little of most things are harmful and are not in alignment with long-term sustainability.

If you feel you can use some help with managing sustainable habits, you can turn to technology to help you effectively balance your health. As you know, these trackers come with warnings; don't overdo it. Don't track your progress so much that you lose balance in other areas. A few trackers you may wish to research are: Fitbit, Fuelband, Jawbone, Apple Health Kit, Fooducate, and Mindful eating.

Leadership

As a leader, good health isn't just important for you; it is also vitally important for your employees. Eating a healthy, balanced diet filled with fruits, vegetables, proteins, and low fats is good for the employees' long-term health, and it's good for the productivity of the employees. This equates to more output per labor hour in your organization. Stepping up and leading the charge in helping your workforce eat a balanced diet creates a win-win-win. You win by getting more productivity, the employees win by feeling better, which means their family wins too.

While we are educating and encouraging our employees to eat healthier food, let's also encourage them to begin or improve their exercise and fitness program. Remember exercise during the day has a direct impact on our ability to concentrate, problem solve, and manage stress. Start leading your employees by making them have lunch and take a walk. Do not allow them to eat at their desks. Allow them an extra fifteen minutes at lunchtime if they are having difficulty managing a walk in addition to lunch. The organization, employee, and their families will gain significant benefits if you make your employees exercise and eat a healthy, well-balanced lunch.

All leaders in the organization should pull a list of their employees together and visit each of them individually. Ask them what obstacles are preventing their walking or taking some other form of exercise at lunchtime. You will hear excuses such as having too much work to do, not having the proper shoes, not having this, not doing that, and so on. Regardless of the obstacle, it's your job, as the leader, to remove obstacles and see to it that your employees develop a sustainable habit of walking at lunchtime and eating a balanced meal for lunch.

Companies Leading with Healthy Habits

Tim Brabender is cochairman of the board of McGohan Brabender, the largest, independent, employee-benefits insurance agency in Ohio. The company has a dynamic culture that promotes work-life balance. It includes promoting exercise and eating a balanced diet. The employee lounge area is filled with fresh fruits, vegetables, and oatmeal for those who forgot to eat breakfast at home. By the way, there is no charge for the food. The healthy food and beverages come with the compliments and encouragement of the leadership team. In addition, McGohan Brabender focuses on offering water as a beverage, not soda. Since water is the best drink to fuel thoughts and rejuvenate the body, it is no surprise this health-conscious organization promotes only the best options for its employees.

The company offers an employee program called *Empowering Healthy Living*. The leadership team believes promoting a healthy, well-balanced diet, coupled with encouragement and time allowed for exercise, will help their employees change their lifestyles to live a healthier, stronger, and more vibrant life. The leadership also understand their employees are more productive, creative, focused, and able to service their client base better than their competitors because they are powered by healthy lifestyle choices.

The University of Dayton (UD) promotes wellness through a balanced diet and fitness program. As an adjunct professor at UD, I often receive e-mails about upcoming fitness programs. The dean of the school of business, my leader, promotes these programs and encourages all staff members to participate. The programs range from learning how to eat a balanced diet, running clubs, walking clubs, yoga, weight training, and meditation. Whether an organization is large or small, providing leadership by educating and encouraging your workforce to get fit is considered a best practice, by today's standards, for all leaders.

There is no company too small to be concerned about the health habits of its workforce. There is an information technology development company down the street from my office. Every day of the week, six of its employees walk a two-mile loop around the neighborhood at 11:00 a.m. At noon, you will see another group of six employees walk the loop. The company has twelve employees, and they take turns leaving the office to ensure adequate phone and online support for their IT customers. It is part of their culture. It is what they do. They do it on sunny and warm days, hot days, and cold and snowy days. Once in a while, you see the group stop at a local eatery to have a quick bite to eat before going back to the walking trail. For a few of the employees, walking at lunchtime does not provide enough exercise, so they peddle their bikes to work.

The Mega Corps May Be Deceiving Their Workforce

Google, a company that most look to as a leader, interestingly, may be deceiving its workforce. While Google and other organizations such as Bloomberg provide healthy snacks, there's an insidious other side to this gesture. If you talk to the employees, they might tell you that part of their company's free, healthy food program is an attempt to get employees to stay at work rather than leave for a lunch break. The continual provision of food also plays into the notion that employees may voluntarily work longer hours and eat while working at their desks. This isn't balance. This is just another way to perpetuate imbalance and maximize the employees' "time on the job" at the expense of long-term consequences of imbalance.

Reflection Activity for Individuals

Oftentimes, some of us are so busy that we skip the opportunity to communicate constructively with ourselves. Learning journals can help you stretch yourself, push the boundaries of your thinking, pose questions, and make meaning out of your work experiences and relationships. Start taking a look at how much time you devote to your healthy habits of proper diet and exercise. Please consider where you could make changes to become more balanced. Take a moment to record some notes in your learning journal or use the space provided.

Reflection Activity for Managers

Take a look at how much time you allot for your employees to devote to exercise. It may be time to evaluate your employees' clock-in and clock-out times. Evaluate the possible effects on your workforce if you were to implement a flex-time schedule. This schedule could support employees who want to exercise in the morning and those who prefer to exercise in the evening.

REFLECTION BOX

Write a note to yourself in this box, briefly describing how you could make some changes so you can continue to eat, or begin eating, a better diet and can exercise more often.

REFLECTION BOX

Write a note to yourself in this box, briefly describing how you could make some changes to your flex-time schedule and what effect you think this could have on the employees.

*"Knowing where you get your worth
from brings inner peace."*

CHAPTER 4

Faith: Honoring Your Values

There is an organization in the United States that starts each day of work with a prayer. This organization is doing wrong by offending people in the organization, according to the political correctness police. I wonder if someone plans to draw up a lawsuit against this organization. Probably not since this is the organization that writes and passes our laws. Below is a copy of the prayer read aloud to all of the leaders and team members on their first day of work on January 5, 2016:

> Merciful God, we give You thanks for giving us another year. We give You thanks also for the first session of the 114th Congress, and Your sustaining us with Your presence, wisdom, patience, and love. We ask that the efforts of the first session might prove fruitful in the benefits redounding to our Nation and its people.

We ask as well Your forgiveness for the smallness of actions on some occasions and the inability to work together when so many were adversely affected. We know that this is not what You wish for us, not what the American people wish for our Nation, and not what the Members of this people's House have been elected for. Lord, have mercy.

We ask Your blessing now on each Member of Congress, that they might be their best selves in representing not only their constituents, but also the entire American citizenry. They have taken oaths to do so. Give them the strength and the wisdom to fulfill those oaths.

We thank You as well for this marvelous forum, where the important business of this Nation has been done in the past and will be done in the upcoming second session. May the work to be done be inspired by the wisdom of prophets and the love of saintly people.

May all that we do be done for Your greater honor and glory. Amen.

—Reverend Patrick J. Conroy, SJ

It appears that one of our country's most prestigious organizations has found time to include faith into its day-to-day work. Since the United States Congress and Senate include faith in the workplace, perhaps we should ponder our belief that the politically correct thing to do is to leave our faith at home.

This chapter is about including faith and religious practices when we are trying to prioritize the ebb and flow of our lives. If we don't set aside time for religious practice, things will eventually go off balance, which can produce unpleasant consequences. Making time for your religious beliefs at home, work, school, and in your social life means you are including them in the balance of your life. Remember, too much or too little of faith, family and friends, career, or health is an out-of-balance and unhealthy formula.

My Bias and Support of All Faiths

Thanks to my parents, I have been and continue to be a *practicing* Catholic Christian since the cradle. Many years ago, my wife decided to leave the marriage. As some of you may have experienced, this was a difficult time for all involved. Since that event, I decided to move forward with my life and remarry. Many of you realize that being divorced and remarried is not necessarily in alignment with the teachings of the Catholic Church, hence my emphasis on being a *practicing* Catholic. I do not put myself out as a saint or as a leader in the church. I strive to live and lead with simple principles and values. I believe in following the spirit of faith, and I try to incorporate these spiritual values in my daily work.

When I was a young Catholic, I thought I was a member of the "only" team. As I matured and learned more about my faith, I realized the Catholic way of teaching is that we need to respect all faiths and religions.

As a leader of an organization, I believe in supporting and being respectful of all faiths. Balancing faith and work is what this chapter is about. It is not about arguing over which faith or religious practice is superior or inferior. It is about being respectful, in words and actions, of all employees' religious faiths.

Faith Matters

There is no doubt that faith matters to a majority of people even though we frequently try to avoid any mention of it in our workplace because it is such a sensitive topic. A 2011 Gallup poll states that 90 percent of American adults say that religion is either very important or fairly important in their lives. Since faith is important in most people's lives, managers and leaders should, perhaps, stop treating the faith needs of employees as a taboo.

I am familiar with the employment laws regarding nondiscrimination in the workplace. Not discriminating against a person's religious preference or practice is protected by law. Some managers and leaders willingly, or perhaps unwillingly, interpret this law to mean that no one can have discussions about religion or faith in the workplace. They could not be further from the truth. Engaging in faith-based conversations is perfectly legal and can help employees understand each other better. If some people wish to remain private about their faith, everyone should respect that too.

Greater understanding and acceptance of each other's faith needs defines the concept of diversity and inclusion. Once an organization learns to appreciate diversity, productivity improvements result from the workforce having a greater respect for each other's needs. For example, when a group of Christians are permitted to take off from work from noon to three on Good Friday, they return to work energized. They express their appreciation of their leaders' recognition of their religious needs through greater effort and output. They no longer struggle to balance faith and work. Their individual goals are no longer in conflict with organizational goals. Having a dialogue with your workforce to understand the important needs of Christian, Jewish, Muslim, Buddhist, and Hindu employees, and of those espousing other religions, is the first step you can take to begin meeting the faith needs of your workforce.

Our religions may vary, but this focus on religion in our personal lives means that there are certain values we have in common: respect, kindness to others, the greater good, and focus on community. If they matter to all of us personally, organizations and society as a whole should continue to honor these values. And yet some leaders continue to lose sight of our collectively agreed morals and values by worshiping Wall Street. Some choose to solely focus on profitability and getting the maximum use out of every resource, including human beings, regardless of the cost to the individual, family, and society.

Be True to Yourself

It's important to stay true to who you are and your faith. I learned this lesson early in my career. I had just started my first job, at Xerox, as a business development representative. A few months passed and I found myself approaching the Christmas season. My sales manager told me that it was not professional to send out cards that had the words *Merry Christmas* on them. He told me we wouldn't want to offend anyone. "Offend anyone?" I said. "What about offending God because you are embarrassed to be true to your beliefs and values?" We did not see eye-to-eye on this subject. I sent out Christmas cards that year and have done so for the past twenty-five years without offending anyone. In fact, some of the recipients of my cards are Jewish and Muslim. They, in turn, send me Happy Hanukkah and Happy Ramadan cards. They are not offended, nor am I. We have a great respect for each other and have learned how much we have in common by staying true to our beliefs.

As employees, we shouldn't feel obligated to work on our religious holidays. We should be able to take that time to reflect. Honoring our personal values and beliefs is the first step we can take to being true to ourselves. If you are a father or mother, this is a great example for your children, who will see how you make your religious practice an important component of your everyday life. Employers who force employees to work on religious holidays, or make them feel very uncomfortable when they take time off on a religious holiday, are another example of how corporate America is eliminating opportunities for spiritual reflection.

Faith and the Workplace: Corporate Examples

Chick-Fil-A. We may think that our modern workplace has no room for faith, but some very successful businesses are proving otherwise. Chick-Fil-A is a leading franchising fast food organization with over 1,700 locations that insists all of its restaurants be closed on Sundays. According to the company website, the founder, Truett Cathy, believes that all franchised Chick-fil-A operators and restaurant employees should have an opportunity to rest, spend time with family and friends, and worship if they choose to do so. He states it is their recipe for success. I and many others agree!

Tyson Foods. This mega-multinational, publicly traded business is known for its faith-friendly corporate culture. In 2016 the Tyson Foods website states the company employs over 115 chaplains to provide compassionate pastoral care and ministry to team members and their families, regardless of their religious or spiritual affiliation or beliefs. I can only imagine the peace of mind the 115,000 employees have regarding balancing their individual faith needs with corporate needs. Congratulations go to Tyson's chairman, John Tyson, and

CEO Donnie Smith for being leaders who demonstrate that *faith-friendly* is alive and producing great benefits to all stakeholders.

PepsiCo. This is another mega-multinational organization that we all know and that awakens our taste buds as we think of popping the top off a can or bottle. Indra Nooyi is a female, foreign-born Fortune 500 CEO who is also a devout Hindu from India. She brings her prayer life and values into the workplace. She has been an avid proponent of helping women balance the demands of being wives, mothers, daughters-in-law, and corporate executives. She explained in a *Hinduism Today* interview how she relies on her faith to bring her back into balance when the stress levels of a demanding schedule become too high.

Faith and the Workplace: My Dad, a Quiet Employee Example

My dad is a retired, second-generation tool and die maker. He began the trade while still in a Catholic high school and worked at it for over fifty years. He perfected his trade over decades and was known as one of the best in the Dayton area. That says a lot about his skills since Dayton was known as the tool and die capital of the world back in his day.

The trade was known to be very challenging, and it won great respect from other trades. Most of his mathematical calculations were written by hand on paper. In his day, there wasn't any software, as there is today, to guide cutting blades and drill presses to make precision cuts within ten-thousandths of an inch.

Consequently, with technology booming over the years, the tool and die trade changed dramatically with the infusion of software-guided cutting machines. The hand-to-eye coordination of a skilled person was no longer needed. After my dad retired, he told me how much he prayed every day. I had no idea he was such a devout person. Granted, during my upbringing, we went to Catholic Mass every week, but talking about prayer or Jesus was not usual in our home. He told me how he became one of the best tool makers in Dayton, "When I had to make a precision cut, I asked Jesus to guide my hands. I turned my work over to Jesus and let him do the work for me."

When he told me that at the kitchen table one morning, during our coffee time, I got goose bumps. I was extremely happy to hear how he had integrated his faith into his work. I have emulated his prayer at work. Though I may not be making precision cuts on steel, I do pray during the day and ask for guidance before I teach, consult, speak, and write.

Tactics to Balance Faith

If religious faith is important to you, make time for it. If you are a Christian and do not want to work on Sundays, discuss your concerns and interest with your manager. Hopefully, that person will be faith friendly and will understand and support your interest. If not, you may end up questioning whether you are a good fit for the company and whether you are exchanging faith-time for profit time. At the end of the day, aligning your personal values with employers' and leaders' corporate values is the number-one tactic to balance faith. Misalignment of personal and corporate values is also the number-one reason for disengagement at work, low employee satisfaction, and high turnover rates.

I highly encourage you, my readers, to understand the balance you are seeking. If you want to follow Truett Cathy's Chic-Fil-A concept of taking time for your religion and family on Sunday, then do so. Don't work on Sundays. Don't work on your religious holidays.

You may think I am making this out to be simpler than it is, and perhaps I am. However, I believe—and statistics favor this belief—that most leaders and managers allow their employees to worship on their given days of celebration. If you are someone who has been sacrificing worship time for clock time, it may be time to talk to your manager. Explaining your religious beliefs and needs ahead of time will more than likely achieve your desired result. If Sunday is your religion's most important day, don't work on Sundays. If Saturday is that day, don't work Saturdays. It is okay to voice your interest in how you wish to worship.

Maybe you are in a difficult situation that does not support keeping your chosen Sabbath. I understand. Life brings us twists and turns that we don't expect or anticipate. I encourage you to continue to honor your faith and values while being respectful of your fellow employees' faiths. If you can't get time off from work to attend your religious service, then choose the next best thing. Go for a walk, get away from it all, and spend your time walking in prayer, meditation, or reflection. This is one of the best ways to clear your mind, reset the faith button inside you, and give yourself a dose of positive energy.

Leadership

As leaders, we are called to honor our employees' faith as well as our own. This can be achieved in a two-step process. First, get to know your employees. What is their family dynamic? What are their interests? Who practices a faith and what kind? Once you have a good understanding of your team members, the second step is about leading. Substitute or allow employees to swap shifts with those who request time off for religious reasons. For example, I always try to take time off from work on Good Friday between the hours of noon and three. I also encourage any other Christian employees to do so who want to take this time for prayer or reflection.

Another leadership tactic is to provide your workforce with flexible scheduling (flex-time) during the day. Allowing flexible arrival and departure times, as well as flexible work breaks, will provide numerous productivity benefits for you while meeting the needs of your workforce. If you have employees who want to leave early, allow them to shorten or exchange meal breaks for an early departure from the office. As leaders and managers, we need to ensure we get the output needed to satisfy customer demand. How we attain this objective defines who we are as leaders. Aspiring to meet the religious, family, and health needs of our workforce by promoting flexibility within our organization is an example of the new genre of leadership: authentic and altruistic leadership.

Authentic and altruistic leaders are genuine in their care and love for their workforce. They are respectful of, and sensitive to, their workforce's needs. These new genre leaders willingly add floating holidays so their workforce can satisfy religious duties without disrupting standard work schedules. If you do not offer one or two floating holidays as an option, this would be a great time to introduce this benefit to your employees and really give them something to celebrate.

(REFLECTION ACTIVITY FOR INDIVIDUALS)
REFLECTION BOX

Write a note to yourself in this box briefly describing how you could integrate your faith and work. Please describe:

(REFLECTION ACTIVITY FOR MANAGERS)
REFLECTION BOX

What can you do as a leader in your organization to help your managers and employees fulfill their faith and religious needs?

*"Fit is simple: transform to your environment,
transform your environment, or find one that fits."*

CHAPTER 5

Career: Finding the Right Fit

"**P**rofessor Hutchinson, I have the perfect future ahead of me," Riley, my fifth-year, MBA accounting student, said during the introductory portion of our first class.

"That's wonderful! Tell me more," I said.

"I just received my official employment offer from one of the Big Four accounting firms! I am starting three months from now—oh, make that three months and two weeks. I don't have to start until I get back from my honeymoon."

"Congratulations on getting married," I said with a smile.

"Two of my dreams are coming true: landing my first choice in a career job and marrying the love of my life, all in the same month. Life can't get any better."

Or can it? I thought. "Hey, Riley, can I see you after class? I have some thoughts to share with you about starting your career."

"Sure, Professor Hutchinson, I would love to talk to you about how I found my fit in my first career job."

After class, I started my conversion with Riley. "So you landed an offer with one of the Big Four accounting firms? You seem very excited to begin a career with such a large firm."

"Yes, I'm so excited to accept the offer. What do you think about it, Professor Hutchinson?"

"Landing and accepting an accounting job at one of the Big Four accounting firms brings prestige and much responsibility," I replied. "Would you be willing to share your thoughts with me about how you are preparing for all of the responsibility and time commitment that comes with the Big Four accounting firms, especially since you are getting married and will begin to share your life with your partner?"

Riley looked puzzled for a moment, gathered his thoughts, and said, "But Professor Hutchinson, this is one of the Big Four accounting firms."

"I understand. It appears to be very prestigious, but this prestige can be quite costly."

"What do you mean?" Riley asked.

"Well Riley, what are the hours you will be working during tax time? How many days a week will you be working?"

"They said we will work between seventy and eighty hours per week and to expect to work every day of the week during tax time. I know that is going to be tough, but all of the firms make the new auditors work that much . . . Professor, that's just the way it is."

The faint voice of Bruce Hornsby started singing in my head . . .

That's just the way it is.
Some things will never change.
That's just the way it is.
Ah, but don't you believe them

This 1986 hit song, "That's Just the Way It Is," plays through my mind when people accept the status quo in any walk of their life or expect me to accept the status quo. "What you just described is culture," I said to Riley. "It doesn't have to be that way," I continued, "but it is what many who have come before you have accepted. You will be told the precedent is set and that's just the way it is. Some things will never change. Ah, but don't you believe them, Riley. Don't you believe them."

Millennials are pushing for change, Gen Xers are wanting the change, and baby boomers are split. Some continue to reward putting the extra time in at the office, and some have begun to reflect and are changing their lives and the lives of their followers. The remaining and retiring boomers are filled with a could've, would've, should've syndrome of wishing they had balanced their lives and the lives of their followers a long time before.

This chapter is about finding the right fit in the organization of your choice. A workplace that is the right fit will promote and encourage you to have balance in all areas of your life. Matching your personal values, goals, and balance desires with an employer and manager's core values and needs will bring greater success in your attempt to achieve balance. On the other hand, if our alignment is off and we do not have a good "fit," we will find ourselves out of balance and unhappy. We can try to balance all we want, but unfortunately, today, many workplaces are frequently "ill" and partly to blame for our balance issues.

Remember, work-life balance will ebb and flow. I do embrace giving your all to your employer for a reasonable period of time. For example, a young, single professional landing an auditor position at one of the Big Four accounting firms could find that position creates the perfect balance. The key to balancing life is to know which areas in your life are in need of balancing. Working and traveling for seventy to eighty hours a week, as a single person, may be perfectly acceptable for that individual's ebb and flow of balance. For example, a majority of public accounting professionals move to the private sector after putting in a few years of grueling work. Their imbalance may have been managed because they were motivated to position themselves for attractive private-sector positions that support most work-life balance initiatives. Paying your dues at the new firm can be in alignment with your goals. Remember it's about finding the right "fit." No one can tell you what the right "fit" is; it is up to you to reflect and discover. Remember to balance your faith, diet, health, and relationship needs when you are burning the candle at both ends during the busy season. Keeping these in balance will carry you through to the finish line. Allowing these elements to bottom out will only cause you to be less effective and productive. Go with the science and go with what those Fortune 500 CEOs do when they incorporate diet and exercise as part of their job description.

Of course, an argument can be made for the *benefits* of imbalance: many of our greatest inventions were discovered by people who were out of balance. I thank these people for their sacrifice, energy, and enthusiasm for their cause, but I didn't write this book for them. I wrote it for those who seek advancement in their careers; happiness with their family, friends, and spiritual pursuits; and a long and healthy life on this earth.

An Imbalanced Profession: Attorneys

We have all heard it before: work smarter not harder. However, that is not the advice of most partners in law firms. The advice they give to new lawyers and their entire team of lawyers is to work harder not smarter. Why? Working smarter means you can do more in less time. Less time means less billable hours. Less billable hours means less revenue and profit. Working harder means more billable time. More revenue and more profit for the partners. Yes, of course the lawyers doing the work share in the money-making machine, but they do so at the major cost of their work-life balance.

It is true that lawyers make a very good living. It is also true they work some of the longest hours, suffer from depression, and are most likely, out of all professions, to commit suicide, according to *Psychology Today*. The journal goes further to suggest lawyers should seek balance in life by taking time to look after their physical, psychological, spiritual, and relationship needs.

Positive Workplace

If the first thing you do in the morning is hit the snooze button over and over, you may not be working in a positive environment. On the other hand, if you wake believing the day is going to be a great one and you're going to enjoy yourself, you are probably working in a positive workplace or are trying to turn your workplace into one.

I think most of us know what a negative work environment is because we have spent many years working in one. Some of us, but not many of us, know what a positive environment feels like. Positive environments energize their workforce. Each and every person brings positive energy to help achieve the mission of the company. Everyone is on the same bus heading in a true north direction. All employees live, breathe, and behave, day in and day out, the positive culture of the organization. When employees and managers wake in the morning, they really do look forward to going to work. Work becomes an extension of themselves, something they are proud of, and they can't wait for the day's journey, which begins by their aligning personal values, interests, and needs with an organization that shares their values and interests and is willing to work with their specific work-life balance needs.

Coaching people in living a life of optimal functioning is the role of positive psychology. The recipe for happiness and well-being, as described by Martin Seligman in his book *Flourish*, can be highly influenced by the workplace environment. Seligman's recipe is PERMA, which stands for positive emotion, engagement, relationships, meaning, and accomplishment. Seligman stated, from an evidence-based scientific perspective, that happiness and well-being can be manufactured by including all parts of PERMA in your life. Working in a positive environment can provide you with several elements of PERMA that you can build on with your other roles in life. For example, working with happy, friendly, and motivated people can give you a shot of positive emotion for the day. Aligning your career interests with your actual day-to-day work can give you a dose of engagement at work. In addition, having a few friends at work makes a positive contribution to your relationships.

Attaining a sense of meaningfulness and accomplishment can, obviously, come from work. Such a benefit can also come from your other roles and enjoyments in life. For instance, taking time away from work to participate in your child's extracurricular activity, or joining a class, group, or club can provide you with a great sense of meaningfulness and accomplishment. It is the combination of practicing PERMA with the various hats you wear in life that may provide you the greatest well-being. Providing your professional services and skills to an employer who supports your balanced life initiatives is one of the greatest paths you can take to achieving happiness and well-being.

Unhappy to Happy

I began studying and teaching positive psychology initiatives five years ago. I was serving as a consultant to a manufacturing company that had expressed an interest in changing its organizational culture. The president of the company was a self-declared pessimist who wanted to create a positive work environment for his employees. I thought this sounded like a mismatched objective, but I thought it would be interesting to give it a go. I explained to him my interests in positive psychology and PERMA. He embraced the idea and asked that I select one of the employees to put together a pilot project before releasing it to the entire workforce.

I selected an engineer named Bruno, who had a lot of personality to go with his analytical skills. Bruno wore his feelings and attitudes on his shirt sleeve. Some days, he was a happy, energetic, productive engineer and a great manager in the organization. Other days, he would be upset over a VP-level decision that he completely disagreed with and did not want to support. Bruno was a great candidate because he embraced positive change and was eager to learn how he could improve himself. I held many meetings with him and, together, we learned about positive psychology and PERMA. We dissected his roles in life and discovered he was not getting an adequate amount of positive emotion and was not enjoying good relationships at work.

Through our many conversations, we developed a plan of action. He was going to seek additional means to receive more positive emotion and enjoy more good relationships. I asked him, "What in life are you passionate about?"

He said, "Well, my wife is number one, and great cigars are number two."

Not being a cigar aficionado, I had a limited understanding of his passion for cigars. He told me he had a friend who owned a cigar shop in Cincinnati and who was looking for someone to help out on a couple of Saturdays each month. Bruno thought this could be a great opportunity for him to receive positive emotion: puffing on a fine cigar and chatting up the clientele who visited the cigar shop. His happiness and well-being surfaced almost immediately.

Because Bruno was able to achieve receiving an ample supply of positive emotion and worthwhile relationships, he was able to be more productive at his primary job. His manufacturing employer supported his working every other Saturday at the cigar shop by not requiring him to work on Saturdays during their peak demand times. His wife was thrilled that he found happiness in the cigar shop and that she had a couple of Saturdays per month to spend with her girlfriends.

We need to remember that employers, leaders, and managers are continually pushed to provide more balanced workplaces and career pursuits. Millennials are leading the charge and demanding that organizations allow them to work smarter instead of harder. They are willing and able to put forth great energy at work. They just want the flexibility to be able to devote to their other roles in life the energy needed for a full and completely balanced life.

It's All about the Core Values Fit

The single most effective ingredient for the success of the employee and employer relationship is the core value fit. Having each other's core values, interests, and needs in alignment creates an organizational commitment that breeds productivity for all involved. All employees, managers, and leaders are pushing in the same direction. They understand the needs of their organization as well as the interests of the individuals (human resources) they recognize as their greatest asset.

I am not advocating that employers accommodate every wish of each individual in the workplace every time a request is made. I am advocating that leaders build a culture that includes adequate accommodation to support individuals' desires and needs to balance their lives. These accommodations by the employer inherently contain restrictions, depending on the type of work the company does and the industries it serves. The key for employees is to align themselves with an organization, including a supervisor who is most similar to them in terms of their balanced life needs and interests. This will greatly enhance their chances of significant success and happiness. From the employer's perspective, it is wise to first hire employees who are a great core value fit with company culture and then teach them the skills they need to perform their duties. According to the *Good to Great* author, Dr. Jim Collins, a leader's task is to find people who are already predisposed to sharing the core values of the company. A majority of scholars also agree it is more productive and profitable to hire for core values fit and then teach skills rather than hire for skills and hope to have a good fit with the company culture.

At the manufacturing company where Bruno worked there was another employee who was a very skilled engineer. His name was Brad. He was a young guy in his late twenties, who had a wife and three young children. He was a promising engineer, quick to understand concepts and issues within the company. He wanted to end his workday at 5:00 p.m. He was a very faithful husband and enjoyed being a dad to his kids. The leadership team looked unfavorably upon his desire to leave at 5:00 p.m. They thought he should stay later and work harder at his job.

Brad laughed at the thought of working harder; he was bothered that the leadership team had no interest in working smarter. For instance, he would complain about having to sit through hours of meetings each week for something he could have received via e-mail. He realized the meeting organizer was a VP who was a controlling leader and enjoyed showcasing his knowledge and others' weaknesses during the staff meetings. Brad found this leadership style to be repulsive and ineffective. His annoyance with this leader and the unproductive staff meetings started to affect his overall well-being and the quality of his work. I approached Brad one day and asked him if he were happy.

"Yes, Donnie, I'm happy," he replied.

I asked again, "Are you happy?"

Brad exhaled and said, "Yes, I'm happy."

I asked once more in a slightly different way: "Are you really happy?"

Brad and I went through this sequence of questions and answers over a dozen times. He finally conceded, "No, I don't think I am happy. I don't fit in here. These guys are complaining that I want to go home to my wife and kids by 5:00 p.m. and that I'm not trying to work hard like the other guys. These other guys are all baby boomers who grew up thinking long hours at work mean more effective work. However, I couldn't disagree more."

"I understand, tell me more."

Brad did not pause for more than a split second. He told me that some of the staff meetings were unproductive and some of the leaders wasted people's time. He was adamant that he could do more work in a standard forty-hour workweek than most of these guys did with fifty-five to sixty hours at work.

"Do you think you will be able to change the leadership and the culture of this company?" I asked.

"No way," he said. "These guys think they are right about everything, and I am one of the few people in the company who wishes to go home at a decent time."

I offered, "Why don't you let me help you become happy? Let's find you an organization that is in better alignment with your balanced life needs and interests. If you work in an organization that supported your balanced life desires, do you think you would be happier?"

"Absolutely. I've never looked at it in the way you just explained it. I would be much happier. I would actually enjoy my family time much more because I would be in their presence in body *and* mind. Right now, I am with them, but I have this nagging guilt feeling that others want me at the office."

Brad left the organization within two months after my talk with him. I ran into him about nine months after he had taken up his new engineering position. He was thrilled. He was very thankful and told me that he had shared his experience about finding the right fit with many people. His engineering career is flourishing, and his family members are grateful for Brad's dedication to them. He is coaching the baseball team of one of his kids and does so with a mind that is free and clear of workplace guilt because he is working with leaders who have similar interests and desires.

Staying True to Yourself

Take time to understand who you really are. I began reflecting on who I was and who I wanted to be when I was nine years old. My moments of reflection began while I was sitting on my sled at the top of the hill behind our apartment complex. I would ride on the sled and play in the snow all day. At night I would take my sled out by myself, walk to the top of the hill, sit down, take in the view, and reflect on my circumstances before I flew down the hill.

As I sat at the top of the hill on my sled, I was higher than the dozen two-story rooftops of the apartments. I could see the smoke coming out of the chimneys, which would rise above the wooded skyline. It was a very peaceful time. The rowdy neighborhood was calm. The sky was clear, and the moon shined enough light that I was not scared.

I realized I was growing up in an economically depressed area. I also realized it was emotionally depressed as well. Very few people I knew expressed any dreams or desires to rise above their circumstances and strive for more. Other kids in our school district made fun of those of us who lived in my apartment buildings. Some of my school friends were not allowed to come down to the apartments to play. When they grew older, they were not allowed to drive us home after a practice or a game. Once in a while, I would feel humiliated and, at other times, sad for the people who judged us.

As I watched the smoke from the chimneys dissipate in the air from atop my sledding hill, I thought about not wanting to become a person who judged others. I thought about how I had learned to not judge others by going to church with my family. Unconsciously, I was beginning to apply what I'd learned from being judged by others in my community. It was at this point in my life that I began practicing the art of reflection.

Every winter, I would return to that hill to sit atop it and reflect. It has become my internal source of reflection. I still close my eyes and feel myself in the presence of that environment. It was through these experiences that I learned a great deal about myself and the person I wanted to be. I learned and understood who I was so that I could manage the challenges of being true to myself. I encourage all of you to do the same. Understand who you really are, and never lose sight of that. You can take this understanding and apply it to finding your right "fit" within an organization. Where is your hilltop reflection sanctuary?

Fit Feels Great

The joy of working in an organization that supports your balanced life desires and needs is refreshing and remarkable. Here are a few lists to help you evaluate culture fit. The first list will help the currently employed evaluate whether or not they are a good fit in their current culture.

CURRENTLY EMPLOYED – EVALUATING FOR CORE VALUE FIT
(To be used by employee and employer)

1 Are the company's values in alignment with your personal values? How are they similar and different?

2 Are the company's vision, mission, and value statements meaningful to you? Are they meaningful to those you work with on a daily basis?

3 Does the leadership team (to include your direct team leader or supervisor) behave in a consistent manner that is in alignment with the company's stated values? Do you behave in a consistent manner that is in alignment with the company's stated values?

4 Do you look forward to coming to work? Are you receiving a good dose of positive emotion from the work environment? In other words, are you having fun?

5 Are you engaged in your work?

6 Do you have enjoyable relationships at work to include your team leader or supervisor?

7 Do you find the work you do meaningful? Is it at least partially fulfilling your need for meaning?

8 Do you find a sense of accomplishment in your work? Does it at least partially fulfill your need for accomplishment?

9 Are you satisfied with your work-life balance? Can you rebalance your workload so you can achieve a more balanced life? Will your team leader and company support this rebalancing initiative?

10 Overall, do you feel like you're a good fit with this organization, and is it helping you with living a balanced life?

Whether you are just beginning your career and advancing it or are on the road to winding it down, finding a good fit requires effort and direct communication. If you find you don't have a good fit, the second list will help you evaluate prospective employers and leaders. I encourage you to ask these questions and really dig into an organizational culture to ensure you have a thorough understanding of it. When you do, you will be able to make a wise decision.

CULTURE FIT QUESTIONNAIRE FOR EMPLOYMENT SEEKERS
(Interviewee asking the interviewer)

1 How do you define the company culture?

2 Please share with me your company's vision, mission, and value statements?

3 Does the organization live by these values? Please explain.

4 Can you give me an example of how you lead and manage with these values in mind?

5 How do you encourage employees to embrace and enhance the culture?

6 Does the company have a culture of its own or does each department or team form their own culture?

7 What impact does culture have on day-to-day operations?

8 What are some of the most common complaints employees make about your company's culture?

9 Could you describe your leadership style? Why do you use this type of style?

10 What methods of your leadership style seem to be the most effective and least effective?

11 What does work-life balance mean to you? How important is a work-life balance for you?

12 Does the company promote a work-life balance? How?

13 Do you as a leader encourage and promote a work-life balance for those you lead? If so, how?

14 How would your employees describe your leadership style?

15 Do you think your leadership style aligns with the company culture and values?

16 How do you handle conflict when it arises?

How Leaders Can Ensure Balance

As a leader of an organization, you set the tone for the culture of your company. In the 2015 Deloitte study released by PR Newswire, 87 percent of business leaders cite organizational culture and employee engagement as their top challenge. Just as a head coach of a sports team sets the code of conduct for the players, a CEO and president set the code of conduct for their entire management team and employees. The buck stops with them. It is their responsibility, and their people look to them to be accountable for the type of culture they inspire and infuse into their workforce.

The millennial workforce is demanding a more balanced life. Generation Xers understand this need and also enjoy a balanced life. Most Generation Xers who are in management and leadership positions are also seeking a balanced life. Baby boomers have a difficult time embracing balance, but if they have an open mind, they can learn and grow from listening to the work-life balance needs of their workforce.

The most critical class I teach at the university and in the field is about helping leaders to understand the true dynamics of their organizational culture. Some organizations have a "talked-about" and "want-to-be" culture. Their leaders' espoused beliefs are frequently expressed in employee and management team meetings. Similarly, statements defining the organization's vision, mission, and values (or guiding principles) can be found posted in some lobbies and employee break rooms. Just because certain values and behaviors are talked about by leadership does not mean the walk matches the talk. It is imperative for a leader to understand if one professes to have a certain vision, mission, and values, one needs to lead through behavior, not just spoken words. This is the behavioral integrity theory that is discussed in leadership studies. As Saint Francis of

Assisi taught, "Preach often, and when necessary, use words." In other words, lead by example.

Two great leadership styles you can learn more about to help ensure balance in your organization are the servant and authentic leadership styles. Servant leaders move obstacles out of the way of their followers. An obstacle in our work-life balance may include our schedule. Learn about the human side of your employees. Find out if they need a flexible schedule. Talk to your leaders to find out what your organization needs to do to embrace flexible schedules so your employees can attend to their personal interests and family needs.

Authentic leadership follows a similar path to that of servant leadership, but its focus is on authenticity. Authentic leaders walk the talk. They get to know their employees very well. If they say they promote a work-life balance, you can bank on it. Truett Cathy and many other executives of major companies exemplify authentic leadership. Cathy began to proclaim, while operating his first restaurant, that the restaurant would be closed on Sundays so the employees and managers could enjoy their families and spend time in worship if they chose to do so. Cathy continued that practice even when the company surpassed two thousand stores and Wall Street proclaimed the company would not be successful if it stayed closed on Sundays. However, Cathy and his leadership team remained true to themselves and have not waivered on their values. That's authentic leadership.

If you are leading a company today, talk to your employees and managers. Seek to understand the roles faith, family, career, and health play in their lives. Search to find what is meaningful to your team. Understand how supporting the employees' and managers' balancing efforts will affect your system. If you ask them in a very sincere and authentic manner, they will tell you. Serve them by meeting their need to balance faith, family, career, and health.

I have a client who decided to do something about the health needs of his staff. His workforce pushes the weighing scales past the categories of one-third obese, one-third overweight, and one-third within the healthy guidelines. The CEO, through the suggestions of several leaders in the company, negotiated a discounted price for employees to join the local gym. He went further by enticing his team with a reimbursement plan: each employee is now reimbursed 25 percent of the cost of gym membership per quarter. There is one caveat. The employees must have their exercise card punched and signed off at the local gym for each visit. If they get their cards punched thirty times per quarter, they receive their reimbursement. This is leadership! This is how you take something that is good for the employees' personal well-being and turn it into a fun and exciting company program and benefit. The employees and the CEO are going to exercise classes together, after work, three days a week. It's very easy to feel the excitement and camaraderie in the air in this organization. Next on their list is encouraging healthy eating. The employees have sponsored this initiative by voluntarily bringing in a variety of fresh fruit to share with their coworkers.

Remember to reflect on the positive work-life balance injections you give your company culture. Once you give your culture a shot of balance and let it gain momentum and sustainability, determine the impact this work-life balance has on your culture and company. Some may argue that their profit did not increase while not recognizing their employee turnover dropped 50 percent. It is important to be mindful of what effects the rebalancing efforts may be achieving by keeping an open mind and searching for positive attributes. If you rebalance the culture of your organization to one that is supportive of work-life balance, you are practically guaranteed a positive impact on your organization and on you as a leader.

Remember to walk the talk. In addition to embracing work-life balance in theory, determine what you could be doing to put action behind your thoughts. Some policy changes may be needed. Some of your old cultural norms may have to be tossed aside to allow new work-life balance norms to thrive. Your culture of work-life balance begins and ends with you. Are you ready to balance?

(REFLECTION ACTIVITY FOR INDIVIDUALS)
REFLECTION BOX

Write a note to yourself in this box briefly describing how good of a fit you feel you have with your current employer. Please describe:

(REFLECTION ACTIVITY FOR MANAGERS)
REFLECTION BOX

Please list the old cultural norms or policy changes that need to be replaced by newer, balanced, work-life practices to help your managers and employees find greater fit. Please describe:

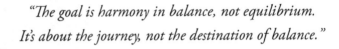

*"The goal is harmony in balance, not equilibrium.
It's about the journey, not the destination of balance."*

CHAPTER 6

Maintaining Balance: The Ongoing Balancing Act

To keep elements of your daily life in balance, you first must know the weight of the elements. Some things require more of your attention than others.

This chapter is about knowing what needs to be rebalanced in your life and how to maintain balance in all of your important roles. If you are someone who subscribes to the philosophy of balancing faith, family, career, and health, it is time to meet this challenge. Remember there is always a need to put more energy into one area of your life than another. **The art of balancing is knowing how to balance the imbalance.** Your balancing needs constantly change depending on where you are at a particular time in your day, week, month, year, and life stage. Just don't let yourself get out of balance for too long because destruction and failure can be the result.

You can't always be in a perfect balance. Busy periods of time necessitate some imbalance. The key is to not extend yourself too long in any one or two directions. I have been going through the challenges of imbalance over the last several months. My drive to finish this book and my heavy engagement in research, consulting, and teaching have led me to wonder if I am failing to "walk the talk." My family reminds me that I'm not failing to "walk the talk," because they know I gave myself and them a deadline by which to correct my imbalance.

Life can, sometimes, appear to be hectic and overwhelming with all of the challenges we face day in and day out. Managing our time and the constant challenge of meeting everyone's needs in addition to our own is a hard route to navigate if we simply don't know which areas of our lives require adjustment. One solution I have found is that when I change my mental model from *having* to do something to *getting* to do something, my view of the challenge changes, and I embrace the task at hand. This is *cognitive restructuring*: attempting to correct the cognitive distortions faced routinely, especially the difficult ones. For example, on Wednesday and Thursday evenings, I used to think that I *had* to drive my younger daughters to their separate extracurricular events. One girl needed to go to cheerleaders' practice or a game, the other to basketball or soccer practice. And I couldn't forget to stop by the school, because one of the two likely forgot to bring her homework. I believe the girls feel I'm their Uber driver. Correction: I feel I'm their Uber driver. However, when I change the *have* lens, the lens through which I view the situation, to a *get to* lens, the dynamics of the situation change. I now embrace the opportunity to Uber them around to their activities. I feel fortunate that I'm involved in this part of their lives. I take advantage of this time to connect with them during the car ride to and from the practices. I also always have something with me that I want to work on for one of my other roles in life. This makes the downtime during the practice sessions on these evenings productive and balanced. For instance, once in a while, my wife will join me, and we will grab a bite to eat, or I will bring my running clothes and shoes to get my exercise in for the day. One way or another, I plan my use of the time wisely to ensure I am maintaining balance in all areas of my life. Don't forget you can use downtime to stop and reflect.

Taking time to reflect while exercising or just sitting still helps me put my imbalance into perspective. For example, though I have been spending a great deal of time with work-related responsibilities, I do schedule time to eat and exercise. I remind myself that proper nutrition and exercise are critical elements of my job as an author, consultant, researcher, professor, husband, and father. I absolutely believe it makes me more productive and emotionally stable through-out the day and evening. I continue to take time for church every Sunday, and I try to spend quality time with my wife and children even though the quantity of time may be leaner. Communicating effectively with your family and friends during periods of imbalance will help you through the imbalance process and on to rebalancing, once you achieve what must get accomplished.

Care Giving for Elderly Parent

If any of you have been responsible for taking care of an elderly parent, you know exactly what I mean by going off-balance for a period of time. Caregiving is hard. It is hard on you, your significant other, your children, your friends, and your employer. It takes up a lot of time, and this time is usually filled with sad emotions, especially if Alzheimer's, or another form of dementia, is present. My friend Laura knows this all too well.

Laura is a wonderful pediatrician, spouse, and mother of three teenagers. She has two brothers, who live on the other side of the country from where she and her mother are located. They were never much help to her. When her father passed away several years ago, Laura started checking in on her mom. Weekly visits became three visits per week, which became daily visits and then two visits a day. She went from thoroughly enjoying her pediatrician practice and her husband and kids to becoming what she felt was almost a full-time caregiver. She was very reluctant to seek outside help because of being a doctor. She felt guilty about letting someone else care for her mother, yet the toll it was taking on her had to stop. She was too far out of balance and for too long of a period of time.

Laura found relief when her brothers arrived to make changes. They took the initiative to help their mom find an assisted-living center that could provide twenty-four-hour care if needed. Laura felt immense relief when she realized she no longer had to be her mother's primary care giver and was allowed to change her life back to the way it used to be. She wanted to regain balance at work and home and in visiting her mother. When she started spending more time at home and at her practice, she realized for the first time how much stress her situation had been putting on her family and coworkers, and she became guilt ridden and sad. She needed to forgive herself. No one was upset at Laura except Laura. At this point, self-forgiveness became the answer.

Forgive Yourself: Press the Reset Button

A large office supply store had a little promotional gadget that I just loved. It was a button, the size of a hockey puck, with a big smiley face on it. When you pressed the button, the smiley face replied in a clear, loud voice, "That was easy." It took me no time to order one of those buttons. I sat it on my desk and told myself that I would use it every time I faced a challenge and took it head-on. The instant gratification I received from this little gadget when it said, "That was easy," was addictive.

One day last fall, my wife noticed I was struggling with something. She did her usual thing of asking me many questions until she finally understood my concern. My life was out of balance because I was spending a lot of time consulting and not as much with my children. She encouraged me to just "fix it." I replied, "If it were easy, I would. I want to spend more time with the kids, but I am being pulled in many directions by clients and teaching."

She said, "Why don't you adjust your schedule and rebalance yourself? It's been a while since you've stepped back, reflected, and took action."

I realized that was what I had to do. I would simply slow my schedule down a bit to find more time for my family.

The following week, I decided I needed to be accountable to myself. I needed to follow the walk-the-talk advice I give my clients. I had defined accountability for some clients as "see it, own it, solve it, and do it." I had the first three parts of my accountability system completed, and now it was time for "do it." I would rebalance myself and implement the new schedule. And that is exactly what I did, but something was still missing.

I found myself not connecting as well as I used to with my children. Something was off. Something was just not right. I shared my thoughts with my wife, and she said, "Go grab your smiley face button off your desk and follow me." She asked me to stand in front of a mirror. She said, "Repeat after me, I am sorry. I forgive you. I forgive the person in the mirror." After I said it, she handed me the smiley button. I pressed it and heard those encouraging words: "That was easy."

For some people, learning to forgive themselves can be very challenging. I am one of those people. We need people around us to say, "Hey, it's okay. We forgive you, and you need to forgive yourself." We need to help each other with self-forgiveness. We must all remember to press the reset button so we can move forward in a positive direction.

Single Parent Balance

Solo parenting employees, managers, and leaders make up nearly fourteen million workers in the American workforce. Whether your circumstances are by choice or a result of divorce, separation, or widowhood, establishing a work-life balance can be very challenging for a single parent. One of the most significant and wickedest negative energy culprits that must be harnessed is guilt.

Guilt is the deadliest destroyer of positive energy and emotion. Some people become immobile and feel useless, a condition that is the illogical result of an event that has already occurred. Falling prey to guilt can be a very easy thing to do. Many solo parents feel guilty about not always being there for their kids because of work commitments. Others may feel guilty about having to say no to their employer's or their child's request. For some, the largest cause of guilt is taking a little time for themselves.

We need to remember, excessive guilt is an illogical and automatic response to such situations. Letting go of guilt can be a very difficult thing to do. Pausing and asking yourself a few questions may help you veer toward the fork in the road labeled "guilt free." If you are feeling guilty about something you did to someone, seek forgiveness and make amends. Then cognitively reconstruct your distorted thoughts, forgive yourself, and hit the reset button. Remember that when you choose to forgive yourself and hit the reset button, your journey in life begins anew. Dr. Steve Maraboli, a motivational speaker and behavioral scientist, once said, "We all make mistakes, have struggles, and even regret things in our past. But you are not your mistakes, you are not your struggles, and you are here *now* with the power to shape your day and your future." In addition, be thankful and proceed with your attitude of gratitude expressed as *I get to* instead of *I have to*. If you are feeling guilty about your circumstances—divorce, for example—ask yourself if you did what any reasonable person of good character would have done. If so, let it go and refuse to think about it any longer. The past is the past. Worry and guilt cannot change past circumstances; they can only affect your life's journey of moving forward. Let it go by hitting the reset button.

Finally, it's very important for solo parents to engage in their social networks of family and friends. Allow those who love you to help you. They want to help. The greatest gift you can give them is the gift of accepting their generosity of time. Allow them to watch the children so you can go to the local exercise club or meet a friend for dinner. If you need to work late at the office to finish a project, call your family and friends for support. It is imperative to squelch guilty feelings and allow yourself to be loved by reaching out to your social network.

Constant Reflection for Individuals

Developing a habit of reflecting on the pros and cons of the day, week, or your general situation can be extremely rewarding for you and those around you. Take the time to constantly reevaluate where you are with balancing the imbalances in your life. You may have embedded a daily walk or exercise routine in your schedule, and you use this time to reflect. Others may reflect just before they retire for the evening. The important thing to accomplish is the action of reflection itself. Take action and be accountable for this reflection. Don't be afraid to look in the mirror and face your reality. Being able to have a straight talk with yourself is a key to finding your reality. Be accountable. **See it, own it, solve it, and do it.** If you can master the art of reflection and apply it to balancing your life, you will maintain your desired work-life balance—guaranteed.

Constant Reflection for Leaders

The single most important thing you can do for your employees, family, friends, and yourself is to lead by example. Take a moment, as an individual, and reread the previous paragraph on reflecting. I want you to master the art of reflection, lead by example, and begin to reflect on what you can do for those you lead and serve.

As a leader, you not only have a responsibility to constantly look at yourself but also at your employees and team members. You have an obligation, as a work-life balanced leader, to see where you can help them. Your millennial employees are seeking work-life balance, whether verbally or silently. The verbal ones are easy to help. The silent ones can slip away as they find an employer who is proactive in meeting their work-life balance needs. Your Gen Xers and baby boomers would love to get some help on rebalancing their lives. Take a day to meet with your employees. Get to know them better as individuals. Discover all of their roles and daily needs so you can guide them toward the path of a balanced life.

Several leaders have told me that they get upset at themselves for letting years go by without helping themselves and their employees manage the challenging task of maintaining a productive work-life balance. One can often look in the rearview mirror and see regret. However, what has happened in the past does not dictate where we are going in the future. Our future is determined by how we alter our course. It can be as easy as a slight adjustment to our rotor.

For example, I love boating, especially cruising on a large lake. Just as the wake of a boat does not decide the direction of the boat, your past actions and inactions do not decide the direction of your leadership or work-life balance. You can make the necessary changes through reflection and leadership examples and through thinking about how you wish to maintain balance once achieved.

As you decide to move toward maintaining work-life balance for you and your employees, remember to forgive yourself for anything in the past that is bothering you and hit the reset button. Observe how you are leading and how you want to lead, and make the necessary adjustments. Be accountable. **See it** (acknowledge the problem), **own it** (take responsibility for it), **solve it** (determine what you can do), **and do it** (take action now).

(REFLECTION ACTIVITY FOR INDIVIDUALS)
REFLECTION BOX

Write a note to yourself in this box, briefly describing how you plan to create and maintain a work-life balance. Which areas in your life do you wish to balance?

(REFLECTION ACTIVITY FOR MANAGERS)
REFLECTION BOX

Write a note to yourself in this box, briefly describing how you plan to take action and help your employees create and maintain a work-life balance.

"Optimize your work-life balance so you can reflect with a proud smile."

CONCLUSION

How to Pull It All Together

Imagine an organization where overtime decreased by 85 percent, profit was up by 16 percent, and the average loss of excessive weight per employee was seventeen pounds. Imagine employee satisfaction pegging off the charts, with employees fully engaged in their work while meeting the needs of each other. All of this can become a reality in your organization if your leaders begin to focus on the work-life balance needs of their employees. Employees are putting stakes into the ground in fulfilling their work-life balance needs. Either their current employer is going to meet their work-life balance requirements or they will begin to find one who does. Therefore, if you are the leader of an organization, it is time to put your stake into the ground and take action.

If you don't have a plan for where you want to go, you will never know if you can make it to your destination. The most important thing you can do for yourself and all those you love is to take action and make a plan. Don't let the moments that matter most slip away.

Don't wake up one day and realize you missed the best parts of your life. Your life's journey does not include a dress rehearsal. You are "live" and on stage 24/7/365. Just as a live stage performance requires guts to perform well, creating a balanced life also takes courageous behavior to make the changes necessary for you to rebalance your life and the lives of those you lead.

If you are leading an organization, you know the difficulties of living a balanced life. You might have focused on your career while other areas in your life took a backseat. You know what you must do. You must take care of yourself by rebalancing your own life before turning to your employees to lead them.

I don't know of any effective leaders who do not want their employees to be more engaged in their work. The formula for employee engagement is very simple and is being defined by the millennials in the workforce: to increase your employees' engagement, increase your engagement in your employees. Spend more time getting to know them and what their interests and needs are as they enter the workforce and progress in their careers. Seek to meet their work-life balance needs, and they in turn will be fully engaged in their work. They will do this because you, the employer, support their being fully engaged in the other parts of their lives. It's a win-win for all involved.

This book has illustrated the importance of balance in everyday life—in your own life and in your employees' lives. The pressures of our current culture and the constant focus on the bottom line means we are frequently overcompensating in certain areas and neglecting others, which leads to problems in both our personal and professional lives. Attaining balance in our life and the lives of those we lead will bring happiness to all involved while improving our organization's productivity.

Do you remember James, my friend from the introductory chapter whose life was completely out of balance? After James gained fifty pounds, was made a partner in his prestigious organization, and started to work six to seven days per week, he became exceptionally stressed, and his family struggled. He wasn't sleeping well at night and barely got time to do anything for himself or the people he loved. Nevertheless, in some cases, God has a way of turning one's life around. For James, it was after he was dismissed from the hospital's emergency room.

He was working on a Saturday afternoon and missing his son's basketball game. He felt bad for letting his family down once again by being too busy at work to join in family activities. While he sat in his office, feeling detached and stressed, an excruciating chest pain took him by surprise. He put a trembling hand to his heart and looked wide-eyed around the room at his coworkers.

An accounting associate called 911, and an ambulance showed up within minutes. Everyone at the office, including James, thought he was having a heart attack. One of the partners called James's wife, Nicole, to inform her that James was being taken by ambulance to the nearest hospital. Nicole and her daughter were at the son's basketball game watching him perform the pregame shooting drills. She nervously flagged the coach down and informed him of what was occurring so he could pull her boy from the warm-up. James's family rushed to the hospital. They couldn't help but fear the worst. They didn't know how long he had.

As Nicole spoke to the nurse at the check-in desk to find out James's room number, the son began running down the hallway to find his dad. Nicole closely followed him, along with her daughter. Panting and out of breath from running up two flights of stairs, the three of them burst open the curtain to discover James resting peacefully in bed. The doctor soon arrived and informed James and his family that he had not had a heart attack. He had experienced chest pain that often resembles a heart attack but is associated with stress. The physician informed James's family that this type of stress attack is a precursor to a heart attack. The doctor was educated about James's work schedule and encouraged him to make changes before he found himself resting six feet under the ground.

James took the physician's advice and made immediate changes. He simply said, "Enough is enough." He began working forty hours per week, eating healthier food, and walking and exercising with his wife. He returned to Sunday worship services with his wife and kids and found a new passion in his life: his family. He got involved with his children's activities and pursued a high-quality, balanced life with more passion than when he had pushed himself to the brink to make partner in his firm. As the great Paul Harvey used to say, "And now you know the rest of the story."

Life is a juggling act; balance is the key to well-being, happiness, and success, both personally and professionally. The balance of career, family, faith, and health needs will ebb and flow continually. There are times when we must work late at the office or leave early to attend to a family need. There are other times when a life event automatically rebalances us—for example, news of a severe health condition that needs immediate attention. However, in our normal daily lives we shouldn't focus too long on one element to the neglect of others or else we will see negative consequences.

Our life and what we include in our life-balancing formula should be recognized for what they are: a living system. What we choose and when we choose to do it has an effect on the things we choose not to do. All components of our behavior are intricately linked to each other. It is important to understand that people desire well-being and happiness, yet don't always know the path to get there. Employers want increased productivity and profit, yet many don't know how to engage the power of balancing their employee's lives.

Your career, family, faith, and health all need to live in balance together. This does not mean equal time for unequal lifestyle components; it does mean balancing your roles in life for ultimate well-being, happiness, and productivity. A balanced life is a successful and rewarding life for you, personally and professionally.

A balanced-life leadership style and workplace will be considered the "new genre" leadership style of the millennial generation. Millennials will soon be overtaking baby boomers to become the largest generation in the workforce. They seek and will find balanced employers because it is their number-one priority. Balance is no longer a nice staple to have in an organizational culture; it has become a must-have table stake. Employees' expectations, a new generation in the workforce, and a globalized workplace are all powerful influences. Workplaces will have to adjust and become more balanced if they wish to remain competitive.

Moving from an imbalanced lifestyle and work environment to a balanced one requires self-reflection. Continual reflection and realignment is key to your maintaining balance for yourself and those you lead. Take action and be accountable for your reflection. Don't be afraid to look into the mirror and face your reality. Don't be afraid to look at your peers, management team, or board of directors. Being able to have a straight talk with yourself and others is the key to change. Be accountable. See it, own it, solve it, and do it. If you can master the art of reflection and apply it to balancing your life, you are well on your way to leading others in your organization to do the same. Well-being, happiness, and increased productivity are the guaranteed by-products of balance.

The New Definition of Success

Reasonable profits, sustainable communities, and healthy employees and families practicing a balanced life form the new definition of effective leadership. Leaders who choose to lead effectively by living a balanced life are on the verge of implementing something great for our country. They are on the verge of implementing work-life balance initiatives in their companies. They will need to change some of the HR policies in their companies. But before they do that, they'll need to change their organization's culture. Key performance indicators (KPIs) for balanced companies will include work-life balance goals they have set for their companies. Leaders will begin to look at their human resources as human beings. They will begin to discover how addressing their employees' interests and needs will lead their workforce to greater employee engagement, a positive influence on productivity and profit.

I wish to leave you with these thoughts. Journey through life with passion and purpose. Know that you are fully embracing all of the people and special moments your life has to offer. Continue, or start, exercising and eating healthy food so you bring a full tank of energy to each day. Love your career, or make a change and do something you love. Attend to your religious needs and allow spirituality to be your guidepost. Know that when you approach the end of your life, you will look back with no regrets. You will look back with your loved ones and smile because you know you made the best of your journey. You balanced your life to enjoy great pleasures on earth. As a leader, you discovered great joy in helping others become balanced so they could reap all of the power, benefits, and success of a balanced life.

Be courageous, my friends. Reflect and take action to begin your new journey.

For All Individuals:

For a *free* work-life balance online assessment with immediate results please visit: www.leadwithbalancebook.com.

For Leaders of Organizations:

For a *free* online assessment with immediate results to discover how well you lead with balance, please visit: www.leadwithbalancebook.com.

For All Readers:

I want to hear from you. I want to know if *Lead with Balance* has had an impact on you as an individual, as a leader, or in your organization. Please email me at donnie@donniehutchinson.com

For All Organizations:

If you are interested in learning more about how work-life balancing strategies could assist you and your organization, please contact me at donnie@donniehutchinson.com.

ABOUT THE AUTHOR

D onnie Hutchinson is a university professor, business consultant, executive coach, and speaker, teaching how leaders who focus on work-life balance substantially increase employee engagement and productivity. Clients have experienced breakthrough sustainable changes through his work-life balance strategies and programs. As a professor at the University of Dayton and a doctoral of leadership student at University of Phoenix, Donnie understands millennials work-life balance requirements. In his career he served as president for three human resource companies and was president and COO of an *Inc. 500* magazine-recognized business, winning this distinction two years in a row. Find out more about how Donnie might assist you individually and your organization at www.donniehutchinson.com.

NOTES

Printed in the USA
CPSIA information can be obtained
at www.ICGtesting.com
JSHW012130141223
53841JS00012B/75

9 781599 326627